SCENES and WALKS
in the Northern
SHAWANGUNKS

illustrated and written by
JACK FAGAN

First Edition, 1998

© 1998 New York-New Jersey Trail Conference, Inc.

Published by the New York-New Jersey Trail Conference
G.P.O. Box 2250, New York NY 10116

Edited by Daniel D. Chazin
Maps and illustrations by the author
   Cover illustration: Below Battlement Terrace
   Rear cover illustration: Viewpoint Along Northeast Ridge
Cover design by Steve Butfilowski
Book design, layout and typography by
   Blair Saldanah Design (www.saldanah.com)
Layout executed entirely on an Apple Macintosh PowerBook Duo 2300c
Printed by Baker Johnson, Inc., Dexter, Michigan
Body text set in ITC Veljovic Book, 10/14.
Headings set in ITC Berkeley Oldstyle.

Library of Congress Cataloging-in-Publication Data
Fagan, Jack, 1932-
     Scenes and walks in the northern Shawangunks / illustrated and
     written by Jack Fagan. – 1st ed.
         p.   cm.
     Includes index.
     ISBN 1-880775-15-8
     1. Hiking – New York (State) – Shawangunk Mountains – Guidebooks.
2. Mountaineering – New York (State) – Shawangunk Mountains –
Guidebooks.   3. Shawangunk Mountains (N.Y.) – Guidebooks.
I. Title.
GV199.42.N652S534 1997
917.47'34 – dc21

CONTENTS

PREFACE

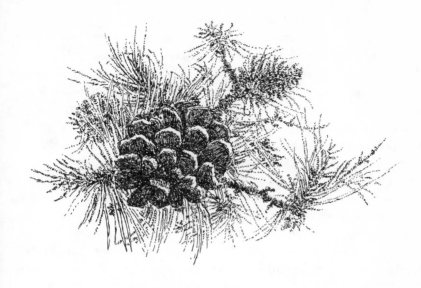

I discovered the Shawangunk Mountains at a very early stage in my long hiking career, and they continue to be my favorite place to walk. In the course of my occupation as a professor of geology and on vacations, I have been able to visit and hike most of the mountain ranges of the United States, and have even been fortunate enough to trek the Alps and the Himalayas. But I always have the desire to return again and again to the Shawangunks, whose unique combination of white rock and dark pines provides for me a place of visual peace.

My first sketch of Shawangunk scenery was done on the cliffs of Verkeerder Kill Falls just over 40 years ago, and hundreds of drawings have followed. Many are reproduced in this book. Some are typical scenes along the principal trails and carriage roads; others are views of less-visited places found off the beaten path. Accompanying my drawings are descriptions of the principal walking routes in the various sections of the Shawangunks, as well as maps and drawings to help clarify the topography and some of the geology. My purposes are to convey a sense of the beauty of this range – with its striking conjunction of white cliffs and dwarf pines – and to assist walkers exploring the mountains to find their own favorite glens and vistas.

I have had considerable editorial assistance from my wife, Linda Lawson Fagan, and from Daniel D. Chazin of the New York-New Jersey Trail Conference. Glenn Hoagland, Director of the Mohonk Preserve, supported the initial idea of this book and put me in touch with the Trail Conference. A number of others were kind enough to read portions of the manuscript – or review copies of some of my drawings and maps – and have made helpful corrections and suggestions. Almost everyone who knows the Shawangunks has their favorite locales, and some suggestions and proposed descriptions were too detailed to be incorporated in a book that is intended as a general survey of the major features of the northern Shawangunk landscape.

I am grateful to all who shared their time and experiences with me. In particular, I wish to thank Tom Cobb, Paul D. Huth, Bob Larsen and Bert Smiley for their review of parts of the manuscript. I also would like to thank Blair Saldanah, who volunteered his services to design the book.

Although I have benefitted considerably from the comments of these and other individuals, any errors in or omissions from the book are solely my responsibility.

Jack Fagan
Kingston, New York
November 1997

OLD MOHONK ENTRANCE

1. INTRODUCTION

GEOGRAPHIC SETTING

New York City lies at the mouth of the Hudson River. In 1609, Henry Hudson sailed north up this wide river in his search for a north-west passage across the continent, a route to the riches of the Indies. Some hundred miles to the north, with salt water turned to fresh and the river narrowing, doubts crowded in. Soon after, he turned around and sailed back south. At this turning point, he was near the foot of the majestic mountains that came to be known as the Catskills.

The Catskills, famous in the Dutch history and legends of the Hudson Valley, became the principal subjects of the Hudson River School of painting. They were the site of many popular resorts or mountain houses of the nineteenth century. This rugged plateau, deeply incised by streams – with heights reaching over 4,200 feet above the Hudson – is still well-known and much visited today by hikers and vacationers.

Lying between the southernmost Catskills and the Hudson River is a less-known mountain area which possesses an extraordinary natural

1

beauty in its unique combination of high cliffs and dwarf pines *(Figure 1-1)*. These mountains are the Shawangunks (pronounced Shongums), or "Gunks." Unlike the broad, irregular spread of the Catskills, the Shawangunks comprise a long, narrow mountain ridge, or in places

Figure 1-1 A typical cliff in the Shawangunks shows the prominent bedding or strata seen in the many ledges and overhangs.

parallel ridges, trending northeast-southwest. They are a northward extension of the Blue Ridge of Pennsylvania and the Kittatinny Ridge of New Jersey, all of which are part of the Appalachian Belt.

Seen from space, the Appalachians appear as a zone of wrinkles or folds in the earth's crust that stretch from Alabama to Newfoundland. Ongoing erosion of the folds has left ridges that vary in height from over 6,000 feet in New Hampshire, North Carolina and Tennessee, to under 1,000 feet in places where the rock is easily eroded. The Shawangunks themselves reach heights of over 2,200 feet. It should be noted that the nearby Catskills lie just outside the Appalachian Belt and do not contain the ridges typical of eroded folds. Additional aspects of Shawangunk geology will be covered in the next chapter.

Descending for a closer look at the geography of the Shawangunks, we see that these mountains lie between two rivers that flow northeast, eventually to merge and join the Hudson at Kingston. These rivers are the Wallkill to the southeast of the mountains and the Rondout to the northwest. Beyond the Rondout rise the foothills of the Catskills. Figure 1-2 shows these two rivers and the Hudson Valley itself. Note the disappearance of the Shawangunk ridges just south of Kingston.

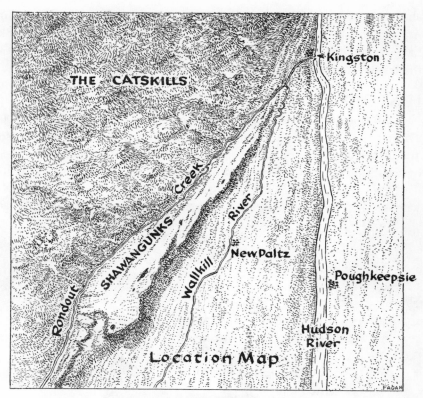

Figure 1-2 *Location map of the Shawangunk Mountains relative to the Hudson Valley and the Catskills.*

Although the Shawangunks extend from the New Jersey border to near Kingston, New York, the most rewarding sections for walking and recreation are between Cragsmoor (near Ellenville) and Rosendale. Just under 20 miles long, this segment – the northern Shawangunks – is the subject of this book.

The northern Shawangunks stand high above the river valleys on either side. The rivers are approximately 300 feet above sea level and the highest elevation in the mountains is 2,289 feet; so the maximum rise is about 2,000 feet in the Shawangunks (as compared to some 4,000 feet for the Catskills). However, the uniquely hard rock of the Shawangunks has allowed the development of much more dramatic cliffs – and more abundant vistas – than in the more famous, neighboring mountains. An addition to the soaring white cliffs is the attraction of the five Sky Lakes – the well-known and magnificent Mohonk and Minnewaska, and the less visited Awosting, Mud Pond and Maratanza *(Figure 1-3)*.

HISTORY

Europeans first arrived in the Shawangunks vicinity in the 1600s. These were the Dutch and the Huguenots who traveled up the Hudson and discovered fertile floodplains along the Wallkill and Rondout Creeks by the mid-1600s. Huguenots built the charming stone houses that still

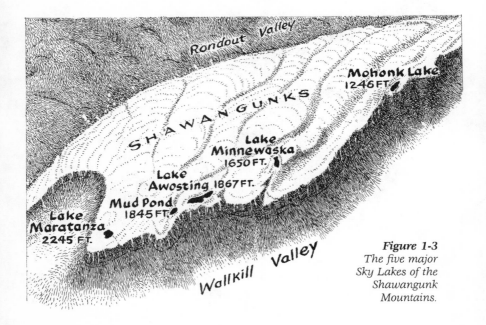

Figure 1-3
*The five major
Sky Lakes of the
Shawangunk
Mountains.*

stand in New Paltz and the surrounding area. They and other Europeans gradually displaced the Indians who had been farming the valleys and hunting in the Shawangunks for centuries. During the following two hundred years, the new inhabitants of the region continued to use the mountains for hunting as well as for fuel and raw materials. Large trees, mostly from the lower slopes, were brought to sawmills to be cut for lumber. Other trees were harvested for the production of charcoal and for the tanning of hides. The hard bedrock of the Shawangunks *(Figure 1-4)* proved to be ideal for use as millstones for grinding corn, and the thin, acidic soil provided an abundance of wild blueberries, which were widely harvested until the 1960s.

Figure 1-4 *Specimen of Shawangunk Conglomerate cut through to show the dense, non-porous nature of the layer. The upper surface, having been exposed to the weather for thousands of years, has become very irregular, with the pebbles standing out. Key shown for scale.*

It was not until the middle of the 19th century that the area began to be recognized for its recreational uses. In 1859, John F. Stokes built a modest structure beside Mohonk Lake that served as a tavern and inn. In 1869, this building, the lake, and some surrounding land was purchased by Albert K. Smiley, a New England Quaker, who was struck by the beauty of the region. The following year, he converted Stokes' tavern into the more sober and serene Mohonk Mountain House. The Mountain House grew yearly, attracting an unusual clientele – mainly well-to-do members of the professional classes, appreciative of its unique natural surroundings.

The Smileys soon began to explore the possibilities at a second Sky Lake five miles away, now called Minnewaska. Here, in 1879, Albert K. Smiley's twin brother, Alfred H., opened another Mountain House, the first of two hotel buildings to perch above this scenic gem of a lake. From the 1870s onward, the Smileys constructed a series of carriage roads astride the Shawangunk Mountains. By the 1920s, a network of these narrow, shale-covered roads had spread over the mountain heights, traversing the woodlands and connecting the Minnewaska and Mohonk Mountain Houses with each other and with a variety of cliff-edge vistas, glens and waterfalls – even with distant Lake Awosting, the third Sky Lake to be owned by the Smileys. Almost all of these splendid old roads may still be traveled by today's walkers *(Figure 1-5)*.

Figure 1-5 *North Lookout Carriage Road. This typical stretch of old carriage road leads through a magnificent hemlock wood towards the Mohonk Mountain House.*

Mohonk Mountain House continues to prosper, although in 1963 a major tract of land was separated from the Smiley estate to become part of the non-profit Mohonk Trust. The Mountain House retained about 2,200 acres, mostly surrounding the hotel and lake. Almost all of these acres are open to walkers by permit. The Trust later became the Mohonk Preserve, which now encompasses some 6,200 acres of the Shawangunks. The Minnewaska Mountain Houses are both gone now, but Lake Minnewaska and Lake Awosting form the scenic core of the Minnewaska State Park Preserve which covers about 12,000 acres of the mountain.

In addition to these three huge sections of the Shawangunks that are accessible to visitors upon payment of a fee, some smaller segments of mountaintop are open to walkers, including a small but important section of Rock Hill owned by Friends of the Shawangunks. South of Minnewaska State Park Preserve lies a 4,600-acre parcel, including Lake Maratanza and Sam's Point, owned by the Village of Ellenville. In late 1996, a 20-year lease on most of this section was acquired by the Open Space Institute in conjunction with the Eastern New York Chapter of the Nature Conservancy.

ACCESS

This book is intended primarily for those who explore the mountains on foot. Bicycles are not allowed on trails or footpaths, and much of the pleasure of discovering the Shawangunks lies in following ledges and streams and scrambling over rocky slopes and through crevices, none of which can be done on a bicycle. However, except for a large area surrounding Mohonk Mountain House and Mohonk Lake, most of the old carriage roads are open to bikers who follow speed and helmet rules and obtain permits.

Originally intended for horse-drawn vehicles, the old carriage roads are superb walking routes, especially for those who prefer level or gently sloping surfaces rather than the more challenging foot trails. In the early days of the Smileys' resorts, few trails existed. As the carriage road network increased, a number of footpaths were developed where hotel guests could make their way up rocky slopes, into crevices, and onto cliff edges unreachable by carriage. These paths, enhanced in places by steps and ladders, acquired identifying names and signboards (Fox Path,

Spring Path, etc.) *(Figure 1-6)*. They were carefully cleared of vegetation but not marked by paint blazes on trees.

Many of the footpaths in the vicinity of Mohonk are still identified by their century-old names on new wooden signs. The Minnewaska State Park Preserve has developed a system of diamond-shaped colored metal

Figure 1-6
Stone steps along Fox Path, which leads up to Sky Top Ridge.

plates which are used mostly on carriage roads. At major intersections, signs have been erected with destinations and distances (some incorrect or confusing). Most trails or footpaths in Minnewaska are marked with colored blazes (red, blue or yellow) on trees, supplemented by cairns (rock piles) where necessary *(Figure 1-7)*. This is also the case on the Mohonk Preserve lands, where a number of useful new signs have also been added in recent years.

The New York-New Jersey Trail Conference regularly updates its trail maps of the Shawangunks. This set of maps may be the most compact source of information available to the hiker. These and other trail maps, as well as descriptions of specific hikes, may be obtained at the Mohonk Preserve Visitor Center. The Mountain House also has available a good hikers' map of its estate and nearby terrain. For the serious hiker, a combination of the Trail Conference maps and several USGS topographic quadrangles of the area make an ideal basis for exploring the northern Shawangunks. These USGS maps are entitled Rosendale, Mohonk Lake, Gardiner, Kerhonkson, Napanoch and Ellenville.

The author hopes that the various maps provided on the pages of this book will prove useful supplements to those mentioned above.

Figure 1-7
A typical cairn (or rock pile) used to mark the trail route in the absence of sizable trees needed for paint blazes.

2. GEOLOGY OF THE SHAWANGUNKS

BEDROCK

The bedrock of the Shawangunk Mountains consists of two geologic formations: the Shawangunk Conglomerate, the cliff former, of Silurian age, and the Martinsburg Formation of Ordovician age.

The Martinsburg is mostly shale. It was laid down about 465 million years ago in a muddy-bottomed Ordovician sea. Layer after layer of clay and silt accumulated for as much as 10,000 feet of thickness. Some millions of years later, these sediments had been hardened into shale. Eventually the sea water disappeared when the region was uplifted as part of an episode of mountain building centered to the east. The cause of uplift will be considered later.

The following period, the Silurian, saw major changes in the region. About 420 million years ago, a shallow sea spread across a rather level landscape of eroded shale. Into this Silurian sea, rivers carried quantities of pebbles and sand grains of quartz which were laid down as gravel layers that would become the Shawangunk Conglomerate. These layers were later

11

buried under piles of younger sediments that accumulated in the ocean above the gravels. The weight of these overlying sediments was part of the process in which the Silurian pebbles and sand were transformed into our Shawangunk Conglomerate *(Figure 2-1)*. This Conglomerate, with its quartz particles held together by a natural "cement" of quartz, is one of the hardest, most durable of rocks *(Figure 1-4)*.

Figure 2-1
*A typical outcrop
of Shawangunk
Conglomerate.
The near-horizontal
layers of rock were
once a series of
gravels that accu-
mulated offshore in
an ancient ocean.*

In contrast to the Ordovician shale, the Silurian conglomerate averages less than 500 feet in total thickness in the northern Shawangunks. Nevertheless, at one time, the shales were completely covered by the conglomerates. Seeing Ordovician shales exposed at the surface indicates that the conglomerate layers have been removed by erosion at that location.

The fact that the shales are seen to lie below the conglomerates in many exposures demonstrates their relative age. To establish an actual age

Geology of the Shawangunks

(e.g., Ordovician) of a sedimentary rock, it is usually necessary to find fossils, especially guide fossils, which are the remains of organisms known to have existed only between certain intervals of time. Fossils are extremely rare in the Shawangunk Conglomerate but are found occasionally in the older shale. The Ordovician fossils include the carbonaceous remains of tiny floating animals called graptolites and the imprint of the shells of small marine animals called brachiopods *(Figure 2-2)*.

When we look at a roadside exposure or outcrop of the Ordovician shale, the most obvious characteristic is the thin bedding, or layering, resulting from the intermittent deposition of original sediment interrupted by quieter intervals of no deposition. When we look at an outcrop of the Silurian conglomerate, the bedding layers are thicker and somewhat less obvious. Also present in the conglomerate are planar cracks, called joints, that are often at right angles to the bedding layers *(Figure 2-3)*. These cracks are essential to the development of the extraordinary crevices typical of the Shawangunk cliff areas, and we will return to them later.

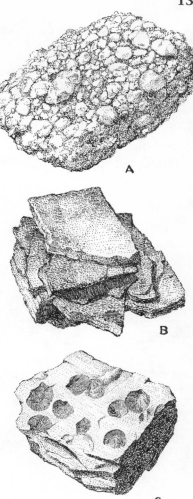

Figure 2-2 *Rock samples from the Shawangunks. A: Shawangunk Conglomerate specimen showing quartz pebbles of various sizes. B: Ordovician shale specimen showing typical thin layers of hardened clay. C: Brachiopod fossils in a siltstone; these are occasionally found interbedded with Ordovician shales.*

FORCES BELOW

Geologists have discovered that the outer part of our planet is broken into more than a dozen great crustal segments, or plates. During billions of years, these plates have slowly migrated across the earth's surface in various directions relative to each other. The movements are driven by forces operating below the crust in the zone called the mantle. At different times, plates have moved apart, collided or slid past one another. Collisions between plates appear to have been the cause of the growth of

Figure 2-3 *Outcrop of Shawangunk Conglomerate. The prominent layering consists of the bedding or strata; and the central, inturned wall (j) is one side of a joint crack.*

mountain chains, and separations of plates have allowed the development of new ocean basins. It is believed that when the crustal plate carrying early North America came into contact with a plate carrying the ancestral land mass of Europe, a long deformed zone, now called the Appalachian belt, was formed by the folding and uplifting of the rocks along the edge of the North American plate.

The first episode of uplift was near the end of the Ordovician Period, about 450 million years ago. A great mountain range formed that was located east of the present Hudson River. Layered rocks, deposited earlier in the Ordovician Period, were deformed into folds. Some of this folding can now be seen in the shale bedrock of the Shawangunk region. Much of the mountain range was worn away over the subsequent millions of years. The sand and pebbles of quartz that constitute the Shawangunk Conglomerate may represent a residue from the erosion of the eastern highlands. A later collision between crustal plates appears to

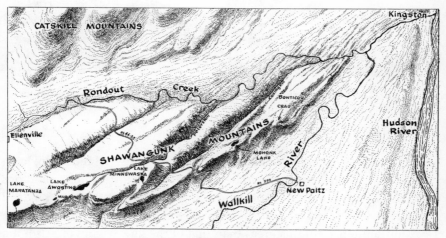

Figure 2-4 *The ridges of the Shawangunk Mountains are formed by erosion of folds or wrinkles in the earth's crust produced by plate movements.*

have been the cause of the late Devonian deformation, about 350 million years ago, that resulted in the uplift that raised the Shawangunk Mountains and caused the folding of the conglomerate layers *(Figure 2-4)*. At that time, another towering mountain range developed; the erosion of those mountains provided the thousands of feet of sand and mud now preserved in the Catskills.

Where plates collide, layered rocks are often warped thousands of feet upward. By this process, beds of rock formed beneath the ocean have been raised thousands of feet above sea level and bent into folds called anticlines and synclines. The more intense the collision, the tighter the folds, *i.e.*, steeper angles of the sides of the folds. Relatively open folds with low angles characterize the Shawangunk Conglomerate,

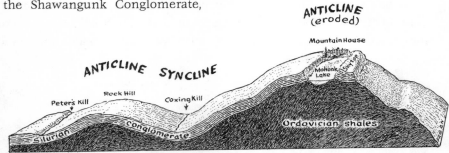

Figure 2-5 *The folded structure of the earth's crust is a principal reason for the ridges and valleys of the Shawangunk area. Faults have been omitted.*

in contrast to the steeper angles of the more tightly folded Ordovician shale seen below the conglomerate and in quarries and outcrops throughout the region. The difference in fold angles in the two kinds of rock reflects the fact that the deformation at the end of the Ordovician was more intense (in this area) than that of the late Devonian. Also, the older shale experienced both collision episodes, whereas the younger conglomerates did not yet exist during the earlier episode.

There are several large folds in the conglomerate of the northern Shawangunks. The Clove, the mountain valley of the Coxing Kill, is a good example of a syncline. Keep in mind that the great size of these folds means that they cannot be recognized in a single outcrop. In the Clove, as you traverse across the valley, you can observe the gradual change in dip (angle) of the conglomerate layers *(Figure 2-5)*.

Once rocks have become hard and brittle, certain kinds of crustal movements may cause them to break along a number of cracks or joints. Usually, joints are parallel to one another. A typical outcrop of

Figure 2-6 *Cliff face above Undercliff Road. Near-vertical joint cracks in addition to near-horizontal bedding plates provide the crevices and ledges that have attracted great numbers of rock climbers to this particular area.*

Shawangunk Conglomerate shows numerous joints, usually at right angles to the bedding layers. These cracks constitute the major planes along which the bedrock tends to break up *(Figure 2-6)*. Water seeping into the joints, freezing and expanding winter after winter, causes a wedging action against the side of the crack. Eventually, separate blocks of rock develop, especially along cliff edges where the blocks are free to inch outward into space and fall *(Figures 2-7 and 2-8)*.

The expansion of cracks, the outward movement, and the tilting of large masses of conglomerate are the fundamental causes of the sharp cliff edges, crevices and pinnacles so strikingly apparent in the Shawangunks. As time passes, the cliffs tend to recede and to accumulate an apron of broken rock fragments, called talus, at their foot *(Figure 2-9)*.

Figure 2-7 *Fragment of conglomerate rock recently fallen from cliff face above Undercliff Road.*

Figure 2-8 *Typical talus accumulation; blocks of conglomerate rock fallen from nearby cliffs.*

Joint cracks are to be seen in almost every rock outcrop. Less common are the rock displacements, called faults, that are breaks in the crust along which rocks slide. In a fault, the rocks may be displaced from a few feet to many miles. Most of the faults found in the Shawangunks show displacements of a few thousand feet or less. The faults cut obliquely across the mountain range; more are found near the northeastern end of the ridges. Faulting is principally responsible for the sheer south front of Bonticou Crag, the break in the cliff line at Trapps, and many of the small valleys that cut across the ridges.

Geology of the Shawangunks

19

MOUNTAINS AND GLACIERS

To what do the Shawangunks owe their height? A number of factors are involved. First, there is the tilt of the layers which are an inheritance from the folded nature of the Appalachian region. Second is the durability and resistance to erosion of the conglomerate rock, compared to adjacent formations of less-resistant rocks. The durability of the conglomerate is due to the hardness and chemical stability of the mineral quartz of which the pebbles and sand grains are made and to the quartz "cement" which holds them together.

In order to visualize the structure of the Shawangunk Mountains in its broadest sense, imagine cutting thousands of feet down into the earth. Here you would find the tilted Shawangunk Conglomerate sandwiched in between the older, underlying shale and younger, overlying layers — mostly of limestone.

Millions of years of slow erosion have left the tilted, durable Shawangunk Conglomerate layers elevated above the surrounding terrain of worn-down older shales and younger limestones. Limestones and shales dissolve and crumble more readily than quartzose rocks; the overlying layers have been eroded down until they are now to be found primarily in the valley of the Rondout Creek. Similarly, underlying layers have been

Figure 2-9 *Stages in the erosion of a cliff of the Shawangunks: A through E. At B and C, ice expansion along joint cracks has caused masses of bedrock to move outward, sliding along bedding planes. Increasing collapse at D and E has resulted in recession of the cliff edge and the accumulation of talus at the cliff base.*

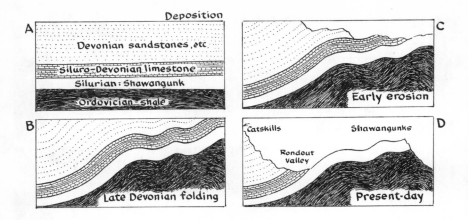

Figure 2-10 *Four stages in the development of the present Shawangunk Mountains: A through D. A: Initial deposition of sediment that became the Ordovician, Silurian and Devonian strata. B: The folding and uplift of the above. C: Early stage of erosion of the folded layers. D: Further erosion, especially of the Siluro-Devonian limestones, to form the Rondout Valley, leaving the more erosion-resistant rocks of the Shawangunks and Catskills as heights above the valley. Diagramatic (not to scale).*

eroded down to the low hills east of the Shawangunk Ridge under the Wallkill Valley. The stages A, B, C and D of Figure 2-10 suggest the gradual evolution of the mountain range.

If you were present about one million years ago just prior to the Pleistocene ice age, you would find much the same general topography as today. However, details of the scenery would be strikingly different. Especially evident would be the absence of the prominent, sharp-edged cliffs and bare rock ridgetops. Long years of rainfall and other weathering processes had crumbled the surfaces until the conglomerate layers were largely concealed by a thick soil.

It was during the last two million years or so that a great ice sheet (like that of modern Antarctica) spread repeatedly from northern Canada southward into the present United States, reaching as far south as Long Island. Each time these Ice Age glaciers advanced across our area, the Shawangunks were buried by ice as much as a mile thick. Picking up fragments of rock from more northerly regions, the ice ground across the ridge, bulldozing the ancient soils and carrying them south. Fragments of the conglomerate were plucked from the ridges, leaving the sharp-edged cliffs.

At the same time, grooves and scratches (striations) were carved on the bedrock by the pebbles and boulders imbedded in the overriding ice. Figure 2-11 depicts a typical glaciated bedrock surface with the approximately north-south trending striations, as well as the curious

Figure 2-11 Diagram illustrating evidence of Ice Age glaciation found on Shawangunk bedrock. Near-parallel scratches (striations) and grooves were cut by boulders imbedded in overriding glacial ice. Chattermarks resulted from collision of these boulders with the bedrock surface. Erratic boulders were carried by the glaciers and left as the ice melted.

crescent-shaped fractures (chattermarks) made by the percussive action of ice-carried boulders. The diagram also shows erratic boulders: pieces of rock carried by the glacier from other parts of the Shawangunks, the Catskills, or elsewhere in New York State. These boulders were let down onto the scoured surfaces as the ice melted away and are now to be found throughout the mountain *(Figure 2-12)*.

The mountaintop lakes of the Shawangunks owe their existence in part to Ice Age glaciers. These lakes are located in bedrock hollows which the overriding ice scoured and possibly deepened. Then, as the glacial ice melted, bouldery debris was deposited across drainage gaps. The resultant damming action backed up waters to form the scenic lakes. Each of these "sky" lakes is fed today by rainwater draining from their surrounding areas.

Figure 2-12 *Glacial boulders or erratics atop glacially smoothed bedrock near Mud Pond.*

Geologists estimate that the last glacial ice sheet melted away from the Shawangunks relatively recently, between 10 to 15 thousand years ago. In the four-billion-year history of the earth, this is but a moment, and, for a rock as hard and durable as quartz conglomerate, there has been very little change since the glaciers disappeared. Thus, the Shawangunk Ridge is one of the very best places in our state to study evidences of glaciation.

Keep in mind that the glaciers did not form the mountains; the mountains were here before the Ice Age. Rather, the glaciers removed the earlier soil from the ridge and exposed the bedrock surfaces, wearing away a relatively small amount of the bared surfaces and sharpening the relief by plucking pieces of rock from the down-glacier side of the mountain.

LOOKING BEYOND AND AHEAD

Since the Ice Age, only a slight amount of erosion has affected the highly resistant quartzose Shawangunk Conglomerate. Striations left on bedrock by the passage of the glaciers are still vivid throughout the mountain and may still be visible thousands of years into the future.

South of our area, the Shawangunk Conglomerate continues to out-crop as a ridge-former. It can be traced to High Point, New Jersey, and across the Delaware Water Gap into Pennsylvania. In that area, the ridge is called the Kittatinny. Although no longer named "Shawangunk," the quartzose strata of Silurian age extend onward as ridge-formers into the southern Appalachians.

Were we to follow the Silurian layers south of the Delaware Water Gap, we would find ourselves in a rather different environment from the Shawangunks. There, south of the zone once covered by Ice Age glaciers, mountaintops are still covered by thicker soil, there are few outcrops and cliffs are less pronounced. In these non-glaciated ridges and valleys, we are seeing a picture of the Shawangunk region prior to the Ice Age.

What will the Shawangunks be like in the distant future? Will vast ice sheets return, as some climatologists predict? If not, we may envision a very slow return to a landscape like that of long ago, prior to glaciation. The landscape of the Shawangunks would return to an appearance similar to that of today's Appalachian ridges south of the Delaware: more soil and less exposed bedrock, with wooded slopes instead of dramatic cliff edges.

3. PLANTS AND ANIMALS

PLANT LIFE

Most visitors to the Shawangunks remember best the white cliffs and the gnarled pines scattered over broad stretches of ridgetop. These trees, so characteristic of our mountains, are Pitch Pines (Pinus rigida). A forest of pitch pines, accompanied by few other tree species, is called a pine barrens. Most pine barrens are associated with sandy soil and low elevations but, in the Shawangunks, Pitch Pines appear to thrive under quite different conditions – there are thousands of acres of pine barrens found here. The pines are one element of the unusual ecosystem that characterizes the Shawangunk Mountains. To understand the development of the plant associations of these mountains, we need to remember the nature of the bedrock itself.

The Shawangunk Conglomerate which makes up the ridgetop exposures and which underlies the thin soils is over 95% quartz (silica). It is almost everywhere solid, dense and non-porous. One of the hardest of rocks, this quartzite conglomerate is more stable and weather-resistant than almost any other type of rock – including granite. The durability of the bedrock means that very little surface breakdown has occurred since

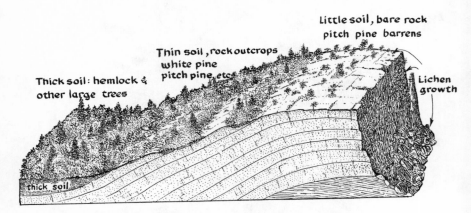

Figure 3-1 *Block diagram of typical ridge, suggesting the relationship between thickness of soil and density and variety of trees. Pine barrens in the Shawangunks occur along ridgetops in areas of thin or absent soil.*

the last Ice Age glaciers melted, leaving broad expanses of scoured bedrock along the mountain crests. In the 12 to 15 thousand years that have passed since, a granite bedrock surface would likely have weathered and crumbled, developing a soil as much as several inches thick. A shale surface would have developed an even thicker soil cover, as can be seen in nearby lowland shale areas. (Angle of slope is another consideration in soil accumulation.) In contrast, most ridgetops of the Shawangunks still display bare rock surfaces or have just begun to develop a thin soil consisting of some quartz particles mixed with humus from plant residues *(Figure 3-1)*.

These new soils tend to be quite acidic, lacking calcium carbonate and other mineral nutrients unavailable in the siliceous bedrock. This is not always uniform throughout the mountains; there may be some variation in soil chemistry and pH because of a local abundance of alien rock fragments brought in by the glaciers. The vast majority of these rocks are less than a few inches in diameter, but some are huge, boulder-sized erratics, often of limestone.

Figure 3-2 *Pitch pine growing on sloping conglomerate surface. Its roots have grown into bedding planes and cracks in the rock.*

Pitch Pines, more than any other trees, are able to prosper on ridgetops with scattered patches of thin soil amid expanses of bare rock *(Figure 3-2)*. They are able to find support and moisture by way of roots tenaciously growing in rock crevices. Such trees grow extremely slowly and often assume fantastic shapes – a kind of natural bonsai. Pitch Pines shorter than a person may be more than a century old.

Elsewhere on the mountaintop where soil is more continuous, though thin, the Pitch Pines grow larger. There they may be mixed with small birches and oaks and a variety of heaths. Somewhat thicker mountain soils typically support taller woods in which White Pine and Sassafras are major additions to the forest cover. At lower elevations, especially in shale areas with more neutral pH and thicker soils, Chestnut Oak, Black Birch and Maples become abundant, and Pitch Pines disappear *(Figure 3-3)*.

For large areas of the Shawangunk Mountains, the dominant vegetation consists of the relatively low growing heaths: mountain laurel, blueberries, etc. One reason for this was the hundreds of fires set in the

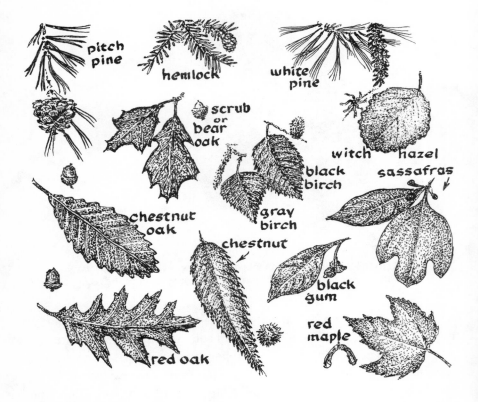

Figure 3-3 The most common trees of the Shawangunks are represented by their leaves. Evergreens are at the top of the illustration.

1800s and in the first half of the 20th century by berry pickers. The yield of blueberries and huckleberries was increased by burning off the tree cover and allowing ashes to accumulate, thereby increasing sun-ripening

Figure 3-4
The evergreen mountain laurel, abundant in the Shawangunks, displays white or pink flowers in June.

and soil fertility. Today, many of these old burned areas are dominated by mountain laurel *(Figure 3-4)*. Much admired for its handsome June flowers, this evergreen shrub has tough, woody branches. The tangled, nearly-impenetrable growth of a stand of mountain laurel can be a serious obstacle to the off-trail explorer.

The rocky Shawangunk ridges are excellent places to examine a variety of the simpler plant forms. The lack of porosity of the quartzite conglomerate makes it almost impervious to water. Rainwater is unable to filter through the near-horizontal rock layers. If it does not sink into joint cracks, moisture will collect on low spots and ledges or will flow over ledges and down cliff faces. Frequently wet surfaces and rock niches provide ideal conditions for a variety of mosses. Ferns are also abundant, especially amid the talus boulders at the shady bases of cliff scarps.

Lichens are quite common in the Shawangunks *(Figure 3-5)*. In fact, most cliff faces and other conglomerate surfaces that appear gray (rather than white) in color are, on closer examination, found to be covered with lichens or the remains of dead lichens, now reduced to scattered black flecks.

A variety of the flat or crustose lichens may be seen on rock surfaces as well as on some trees. In addition, there are several species of Rock Tripe, representing the foliose category of lichen. These leathery-

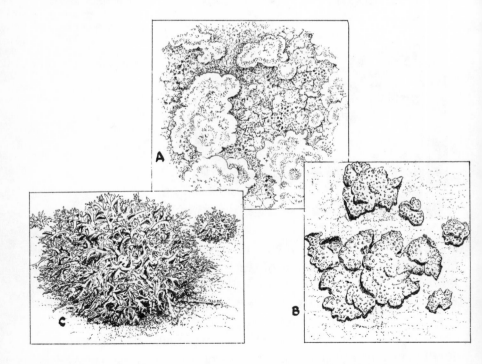

Figure 3-5 *Varieties of lichen found in the Shawangunks:*
A. most common: crustose lichen.
B. foliose (Rock Tripe)
C. fruticose (Reindeer "Moss")

looking forms are usually found adhering to vertical surfaces. Less abundant is the fruticose lichen called Reindeer Moss, consisting of spongy, complexly-branched bundles. This lichen can be found growing on undisturbed ground and on some level rock surfaces. Slow-growing and fragile, both the tripe and reindeer forms are becoming uncommon except in little-used parts of the Shawangunks where they can live undisturbed by hikers and climbers.

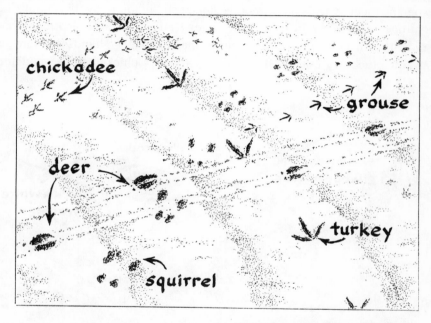

Figure 3-6 *Snow tracks.*

ANIMAL LIFE

The type of animal that may be encountered on a Shawangunk walk depends upon the nature of the terrain. Creatures likely to be found on a rocky ridgetop, on the floor of a hemlock forest, or on a laurel-covered slope may be quite different. Animal activities also vary greatly from season to season and even with time of day. On the average walk along a Shawangunk trail, one may expect to see several species of birds, hear the chipping sound of a chipmunk, or perhaps sense the rustle of a busy squirrel or a fleeing deer. But for the quiet and observant visitor, able to move stealthily and willing to remain still for long minutes, and preferably equipped with binoculars, much more is to be seen. For such an observer, the Shawangunks is a stage full of animal species small and large. Winter is a special time when animals leave a record of their passage in the form of tracks in the snow *(Figure 3-6)*.

Bird life of this area is especially variable with the season and with specific locale *(Figure 3-7)*. Woodpeckers, usually found by their knocking sounds, include the little Downy, larger Hairy and the less-common but magnificent Pileated. On the ground, the Towhee is a handsome forager in low blueberry bushes. The Ruffed Grouse, a chicken-sized woodland

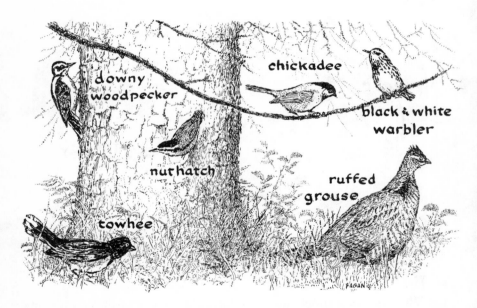

Figure 3-7 *A sample of the birds of the Shawangunks. Dozens of other species may be seen, depending on season and time spent on observation.*

bird, is usually seen only as it explodes noisily upward in flight. Another reluctant flyer is the large and stately wild Turkey, now increasing in numbers each year. Dozens of species of smaller birds have been identified in the Shawangunks, many breeding and some passing through.

Familiar to winter hikers are the Chickadee and the Nuthatch, both year-round natives. A number of warbler species breed here, including the Black and White Warbler and the Common Yellowthroat.

Larger birds, likely to be seen soaring overhead, include the Red-Tailed Hawk, the scavenging Turkey Vulture and – increasingly – the Raven; both of the latter nest at remote cliff sites. During the fall, several viewpoints along the cliffs are used by hawk-watchers to count the hundreds of hawks and other raptors taking advantage of rising air currents along the Shawangunk escarpment on their migration route south *(Figure 3-8)*.

Figure 3-8
A variety of raptors may be seen soaring above Shawangunk ridges and migrating southward in the fall. Among these are the Turkey Vulture (T), the Red-Tailed Hawk (R), and several species of accipiters (C).

Most abundant among mammals of the Shawangunks are the rarely-seen mice shrews and moles. These small animals lead hidden, often nocturnal lives, inhabiting burrows or using the woodland debris for shelter. Somewhat larger and more active in daylight are the chipmunks and squirrels (Gray, Red and Flying) and Cottontail Rabbit. Porcupines are occasionally encountered, usually climbing trees when disturbed. Fishers, weasel-like carnivores, were re-introduced in the Shawangunks some 20 years ago to help control the porcupines, which destroy trees by eating the bark. From time to time, beavers have lived

Figure 3-9
*Beaver-cut tree stumps.
These trees bearing the
characteristic marks
of beaver's teeth were
found along the shore
of Lake Awosting.*

along the streams and in some of the Sky Lakes. Their lodges can be seen at Lake Awosting and Mud Pond; beaver-cut trees are common around these lakes and at many wetland sites *(Figure 3-9)*. Muskrats build lodges somewhat similar to those of beaver – an old example can be seen at Duck Pond.

Several kinds of larger mammals inhabit the Shawangunks. Among these, the Bobcat and Coyote are rarely seen. Bobcats live primarily on rodents; coyotes feed opportunistically, eating berries, rodents or carrion. The widespread growth of blueberries and huckleberries may be a major drawing card for Black Bears which have been seen on occasion throughout the Shawangunks, usually by solitary walkers *(Figure 3-10)*.

Perhaps the most pleasing of animal sightings for many visitors are those of White-Tailed Deer. These browsers, the largest animals likely to be encountered along Shawangunk trails, are most common in areas of overgrown fields, such as those near Spring Farm, Glory Hill and the old golf course at Minnewaska. The white-tailed deer, although native to New York State, were so hunted in the last century that they were eliminated from the Shawangunk region. Their return was welcomed by lovers of wildlife. Ironically, however, deer numbers have now reached an undesirable level and constitute a growing problem.

Figure 3-10
*Black Bear as seen by the author
in June 1994 along the southeast side
of Sky Top Ridge. Bears live in the
Shawangunks but avoid most popular
areas and are seen but rarely.*

Reptile and amphibians of the Shawangunks are not to be seen in the colder months. During the rest of the year, however, it is not unusual to see turtles sunning themselves along the margins of lakes and wet areas. Spotted and Painted Turtles seem to be most common. Snakes have the same habit of sunning themselves, but on rock surfaces. However, the most common snake of the Shawangunks, the Black Rat Snake, often chooses sunny spots on carriage roads, startling walkers and bikers *(Figure 3-11)*. This is a harmless species, like most snakes. The potentially dangerous Timber Rattlesnake and the Copperhead are occasionally encountered in the mountains; they are not very aggressive and will do their best to avoid walkers.

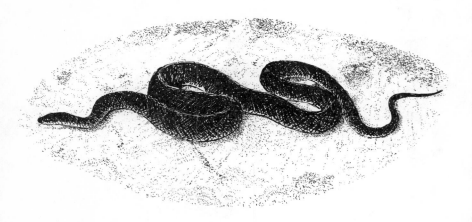

Figure 3-11 *The Black Rat Snake. This is one of the most common snakes in the Shawangunks and is harmless to humans.*

Amphibians are most common in wetland areas. First to announce their presence in earliest spring are tiny frogs called Spring Peepers, which gather in choral groups in ponds and small vernal pools not long after snows have melted. Other frogs, as well as salamanders, may be found by the careful observer along lake margins and other moist areas. Often seen in spring and summer are Red Efts *(Figure 3-12)*. These

***Figure* 3-12** *Red Efts. Averaging a few inches in length, these orange-red amphibians are frequently seen along Shawangunk paths.*

interesting little animals (the terrestrial stage of an otherwise aquatic newt) are sometimes so abundant on damp stretches of old road or trail that they can scarcely be avoided.

It should be kept in mind that most animals (other than insects) tend to hide or move away from the sound of human intrusion, so that a solitary or relatively silent hiker is much more likely to come upon wildlife than is a convivial group of walkers.

4. BONTICOU: THE NORTHERN SECTION

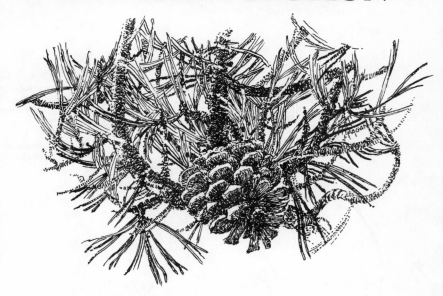

BONTICOU CRAG

Bonticou Crag dominates the ridge line of the northernmost section of the Shawangunks. The ridge-forming conglomerates may be traced as far north as Rosendale, where the strata (rock layers) have decreased in number until the entire thickness is less than 100 feet. The Rondout Creek, which has flowed along the western boundary of the mountain range, turns east and cuts through the conglomerates in the village of Rosendale. The Bonticou section has many miles of old shale carriage roads and marked trails leading through pleasant woods, past old stone walls, and along conglomerate ridges. Bonticou Crag itself, a magnet for walkers, offers spectacular views. The route up its western face is the most challenging trail in this area.

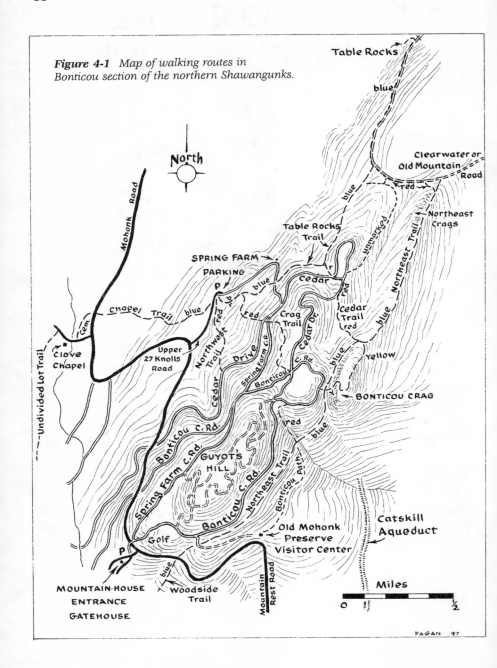

Figure 4-1 *Map of walking routes in Bonticou section of the northern Shawangunks.*

ACCESS

The Bonticou Crag area is the most northerly region of the Shawangunks that is readily accessible for public use. It is bounded by Clearwater Road (formerly known as Old Mountain Road) on the north, Mountain Rest and Mohonk Roads on the south, Mossy Brook Road on the west, and Springtown Road or the Catskill Aqueduct to the east (*Figure 4-1*). Most of this land is part of the Mohonk Preserve which, for a modest fee, is open to walkers, bicyclists, horseback riders and skiers. Parking has long been available on Mountain Rest Road near the Preserve Visitor Center. This Center will close by 1998 and move to a new location on Route 44-55 near the Trapps. It is uncertain at this time whether any parking near the old Visitor Center will be possible after 1997. It is also possible to park at Spring Farm, which is located at the end of Upper 27 Knolls Road, just off Mohonk Road, about 1½ miles west of the Visitor Center.

CARRIAGE ROADS

There are four old roads built for horse and carriage travel in this section: **Bonticou** and **Spring Farm Carriage Roads, Cedar Drive** and **Guyot Hill Road.** Bonticou Carriage Road, Cedar Drive and Guyot Hill Road were laid out in 1882 as the popularity of Mohonk Mountain House grew and its use of the landscape expanded. Cedar Drive and Bonticou Carriage Road were extended further north in the early 1900s. The last loop of Cedar Drive is the most northerly of all the carriage roads built by the Mohonk proprietors. Spring Farm Carriage Road provided access from Spring Farm, which predates the Mountain House.

Bonticou Carriage Road, passing near the Mohonk Preserve Visitor Center on Mountain Rest Road, is a major access route for this area of the Shawangunks. From the old Visitor Center, the Link, a shale lane (yellow blazes), rises steeply for a third of a mile to reach Bonticou Road. The visitor should turn right onto the carriage road to avoid the Mohonk Golf Course (to the left) and head toward Bonticou Crag. (The Mohonk Golf Course is off-limits to hikers from April to November.) The level road passes through mixed second-growth forest. Breaks in the trees allow views across the meadows below and out to the Wallkill Valley.

In less than a mile, there is a complex intersection. A left fork heading downhill is Cedar Drive. A sharp left leads up onto Guyot Hill. Bonticou Carriage Road continues ahead to the right. Beyond this intersection is the terminus of the red-blazed Bonticou Path, a trail leading back to the Visitor Center. Bonticou Road continues toward the Bonticou Crag outcrop which now looms through the trees. Soon a splendid view of the Crag appears *(Figure 4-2)*. Huge blocks of white rock fallen from its heights make a formidable landscape. A yellow-blazed trail leads from the comfortable, level carriage road toward the chaos of boulders.

The carriage road, designed for contemplative views rather than physical challenges, continues past the view and loops back toward the west and another meeting with Cedar Drive *(Figure 4-3)*. At this intersec-

Figure 4-2 *Bonticou Crag from the Northeast Trail at its western base. The Bonticou Ascent Path rises nearby.*

tion also is the terminus of the red-blazed Crag Trail, which leads toward Spring Farm. On the west side of the ridge now, Bonticou Carriage Road crosses Spring Farm Road diagonally and heads toward Mohonk Road. Crossing to the south side of this rural highway, Bonticou Road continues to Glen Anna. The convoluted knot of roads and paths crossing this glen provides many routes for hiking in the Mohonk Lake section of the Shawangunks. Bicycles are limited to the carriage roads on the lower shoulders of the ridge.

Figure 4-3
Fall scene
along carriage
road near
Spring Farm.

Guyot Hill and Guyot Hill Road were named for Arnold Guyot, Professor of Geography and Geology at Princeton, who visited Mohonk about 1871. Guyot Hill is rather a surprise. At 1,270 feet above sea level, it is the highest point in this part of the Shawangunks. It is made not of the durable, white conglomerate that we associate with ridge tops but of the softer Ordovician shales. The conglomerate layers that once covered the shales of Guyot Hill were removed by long-term erosional processes. The very last of the white layers were probably carried off by the Ice Age glaciers.

Lacking bare ledges or dramatic cliffs, Guyot Hill seems unloved and seldom visited today. Still, the old road that wanders up its slopes offers a mildly aerobic climb, with several switchbacks for maximum coverage of its wooded summit. On a bicycle or skis, it is quite a challenge. Access is from the first Bonticou-Cedar Drive intersection.

Cedar Drive, like Bonticou Carriage Road, was a long and important avenue that once allowed guests of the mountain houses, traveling by horse and carriage, to visit the northern area of the ridge and especially the base of Bonticou Crag. Each of these roads skirts Guyot Hill and offers occasional views of both the Wallkill and Rondout sides of the ridge. In the early days of the carriage roads, the vistas were more extensive. Much of the forest had been cleared for timber or to create fields and meadows. With the regrowth of the forests, we can no longer appreciate the views that our predecessors enjoyed. But today's woodland provides a compensating beauty of its own *(Figure 4-4)*.

South of the Crag region, Cedar Drive is lower on the ridge than Bonticou Carriage Road. It is interrupted at Mohonk Road, where a wooden bridge was long ago removed and, again, further south, there is a gap at the crossing of Glen Anna. The high, wooden bridge that once spanned the gorge is gone, and the traveller is faced with negotiating the steep slopes of the stream. These should not deter the walker, but it makes bicycling or skiing undesirable on this part of Cedar Drive.

Spring Farm Carriage Road was constructed to allow riders from the Mountain Rest area to reach Spring Farm. The farm is part of the Mohonk Preserve, but the old farmhouse is maintained as a private residence. Walkers should use marked trails to avoid the buildings. The fields

Figure 4-4 *Ruins along Cedar Drive at its intersection with Spring Farm Carriage Road.*

around Spring Farm are mowed every few years to maintain the historic agricultural aspect. In summer, the meadows are full of wildflowers, butterflies, and those birds that prefer fields and woodland edges. On some summer days, the area is full of day campers as well, pursuing nature study and crafts at Camp Peregrine.

Spring Farm Carriage Road, south of its intersection with Cedar Drive, is used by bicyclists, skiers, and occasionally by hikers as part of circular walks that include other roads and trails.

TRAILS

The carriage roads of the Shawangunks were built for easy horse travel. Many walkers as well as bicyclists and skiers are grateful for these level and gently graded routes through the forest. The trails, however, are walking routes, intended for foot traffic only. They are steeper and narrower than the carriage roads and usually offer more solitude *(Figure 4-5)*. A few require rock scrambling and are best attempted by experienced hikers wearing sturdy footgear.

There are eight marked trails in the Bonticou section of the Shawangunks, all maintained by Mohonk Preserve. Each is marked with red, blue or yellow blazes on trees or rocks. Four radiate out from the parking area at Spring Farm, two start near the old Visitor Center, and two more provide access to Bonticou Crag from other routes. In general,

Figure 4-5 Along the Northeast Trail just northeast of Bonticou Crag.

blue trails follow the approximately north-south trend of the ridge. Red trails run roughly perpendicular to the ridge, and yellow trails are short links between trails and/or carriage roads *(see map: Figure 4-1).*

TRAILS FROM SPRING FARM

There are two blue trails and two red trails that begin at the Spring Farm parking area at the end of Upper 27 Knolls Road. The longest of these is the blue-blazed **Table Rocks Trail.** Across the farm road from the parking area, the trail heads north (left), paralleling the dirt road. Soon the red-blazed Crag Trail goes off to the right, and the Table Rocks Trail turns deeper into the meadows. The Catskill Mountains seen from the meadows seem very close by. Crossing the dog-leg of Spring Farm Road, the trail heads into the woods, passes the start of the red-blazed Cedar Trail, and skirts the northernmost meadow before reaching Clearwater Road (Old Mountain Road on some maps). It is about 1½ miles from the parking area to this point. The blue trail joins the old dirt road and turns downhill through the forest. About a mile down the hillside, boulders of white rock appear alongside the road, the first sign that a conglomerate outcrop is nearby. Soon the blue blazes lead off the road to the left (west) toward the outcrops and up onto the Table Rocks. From the Rocks, there is a fine view to the west. This unique spot, a massive expanse of Shawangunk conglomerate, is criss-crossed by deep fissures and bordered by dramatic cliffs *(Figure 4-6).*

Figure 4-6 Table Rocks.

A gate across Clearwater Road just north of Table Rocks marks the Preserve's boundary; beyond is private property. It is about 2½ miles back to the Spring Farm parking area via the same route.

Chapel Trail is the other blue-blazed path from Spring Farm. It begins along Upper 27 Knolls Road, heads southwest across a meadow and descends through the woods. After crossing Mohonk Road, the trail skirts a small cemetery. Here lies John F. Stokes, who sold the Mohonk Lake property to Albert Smiley in 1869 *(Figure 4-7)*. The Chapel Trail ends on Clove Road across from the charming little church with its vertical board-and-batten siding *(Figure 4-8)*. Just downhill from the chapel is the northern terminus of the Undivided Lot Trail, which leads south into the Laurel Ledge region of Mohonk.

Figure 4-7 *Grave of John Stokes, original owner of the first building of the Mohonk Mountain House.*

Northwest Trail, red-blazed, is a third path that starts at the Spring Farm parking area. From the farm road, it heads south (right) across the meadow and climbs to meet Cedar Drive in about 0.6 mile. This short route was established to allow hikers from Spring Farm to reach areas south of Mohonk Road, such as Rock Rifts and Glen Anna, via Cedar Drive.

Crag Trail is the other red-blazed trail here. It briefly follows the beginning of the blue-blazed Table Rocks Trail but soon turns east, rising through the meadows. Entering the woods, it crosses Cedar Drive and Spring Farm Carriage Road in quick succession. The trail continues to climb through mixed hardwood forest to end at the intersection of Bonticou Carriage Road and Cedar Drive, about one mile from the Spring Farm parking area and about one-quarter of a mile from Bonticou Crag.

TRAILS FROM THE OLD VISITOR CENTER

The old Mohonk Preserve Visitor Center is on an east-facing shale shoulder of the Shawangunk Ridge, about half a mile down Mountain Rest Road from the Gatehouse, the entrance to the Mohonk Mountain House. The building originated as a club house for the golf course of the Mohonk Mountain House. It had been made available to the Mohonk Preserve for offices, although the Mountain House retained ownership of the building and most of the adjacent meadows.

Figure 4-8
Clove Chapel,
at the end of
the Chapel
Trail.

The Link, constructed originally to connect the Mohonk resort with the ski center, has a steeper gradient than the typical carriage road. The Link, yellow-blazed, afforded access from the Visitor Center to Bonticou Carriage Road and the Northeast Trail.

Bonticou Path, red-blazed, starts at the old Visitor Center and heads northeast, downhill along the edge of a field. A splendid view of Bonticou Crag looms ahead. Passing the short Pond Loop Trail (blue),

Bonticou Path enters the woods, ascends a forested glen, and crosses the Northeast Trail. It ends at the Bonticou Carriage Road about 0.9 mile from the old Visitor Center.

Figure 4-9 *Rock pinnacle along southern base of Bonticou Crag, near Northeast Trail.*

Northeast Trail, marked blue, is one of the longest footpaths in this section. The southern terminus of the trail may be reached by taking The Link from the old Visitor Center. From the Link (dirt road), the blue-blazed Northeast Trail starts sharply uphill to the right (north) and heads through a sloping forest. This is not an especially direct route for northbound hikers; most prefer to begin on the red-blazed Bonticou Path and turn onto the Northeast Trail where they intersect *(see map)*. North of Bonticou Path, the Northeast Trail crosses several small stream courses and approaches the edge of a mass of boulders and pinnacles *(Figure 4-9)*. The talus has fallen from the cliffs of Bonticou Crag, now seen high above the trail.

An intersection with the yellow-blazed Bonticou Ascent Path is encountered about 1¼ miles from the Link, or about one mile from the old Visitor Center via the Bonticou Path/Northeast Trail combination. The blue trail continues north, skirting the boulders and ledges below the Crag. After passing the Cedar Trail (red) coming in from the west, the Northeast Trail immediately turns toward the ridge and climbs briefly but steeply to meet the northern end of the Bonticou Crag Path (yellow). Note the range of pebble sizes in the conglomerate layers in this outcrop.

The Northeast Trail swings north again and follows the wooded ridgetop *(Figures 4-10 and 4-11)*. Occasional views are found along the ridge, with those to the northwest becoming more frequent and spectacular. Near the north end of this trail, about two miles from the Visitor

Figure 4-10 Northeast Crags, a viewpoint toward the Catskills, along the Northeast Trail.

Center, there are open ledges – the Northeast Crags – with an especially striking view of the Catskills.

   In another eighth of a mile, the Northeast Trail ends at Clearwater Road (Old Mountain Road). By turning east on this dirt road, one can eventually reach Springtown Road north of New Paltz, but the road crosses private property and is not maintained. To the west (left), Clearwater

Figure 4-11 *Talus at the base of the Northeast Ridge. The person near the top is on the Northeast Trail.*

Road, now marked with red blazes, winds its way past old stone walls and a ruined building *(Figure 4-12)* to reach the Table Rocks Trail, three-quarters of a mile away. For many years, there was extensive flooding near the end of the Northeast Trail, where a small stream had backed up onto

Figure 4-12 *Ruined building along Clearwater Road.*

the old road. Recent rechanelling and levee construction by the Mohonk Preserve has drained this swampy area, and the Clearwater Road now crosses the stream on a wide but simple bridge. In addition to this route, a short red-blazed segment of trail bypasses this bridge and leads upstream across two small footbridges, angling back to intersect the old road a short distance west of the flood-prone section. With the improvement and marking of Clearwater Road, it is now possible to do a circular hike, using parts of the Table Rocks, Northeast and Cedar Trails.

OTHER TRAILS

The yellow-blazed **Bonticou Ascent Path** provides access to the summit of Bonticou Crag, the most visited spot in this section of the mountains. At nearly 1,200 feet above sea level, the pine-fringed white rock summit and its adjacent cliff scarp comprise a splendid example of Shawangunk scenery *(Figure 4-13)*.

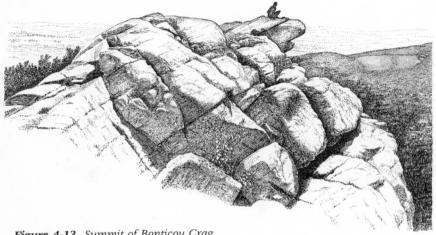

Figure 4-13 *Summit of Bonticou Crag.*

The southern end of this path begins on the Bonticou Carriage Road at a sign indicating "Bonticou Ascent Path." This well-worn trail heads downhill for a short distance, crosses the Northeast Trail and heads up through a great rock pile at the base of the Crag. Scrambling its way over giant talus fragments, the steepening trail reaches a near-vertical cliff which it ascends via ledges and cracks to the crest of the Crag. This short climb requires the use of hands as well as feet, and should be negotiated with caution. At the broad summit of the Crag, the reward is great. On a clear day, there are views northwest to the Catskills, northeast to Stissing Mountain and Dutchess County, and southeast to the Hudson Highlands.

Heading north from the Crag top, the yellow trail is at first difficult to pick out from among the several tracks worn by visitors to this popular mountaintop spot. The path descends through mixed forest over conglomerate outcrops, occasionally with more views toward the southeast and northwest. The northern terminus of the Bonticou Ascent Path is an intersection with the Northeast Trail (blue) where the latter ascends from the base of the cliff to the ridgetop.

The total length of the Bonticou Ascent Path is less than three-fourths of a mile. Because of its challenges, it seems longer to most hikers. It must be noted that the views from the Crag are just as fine for those who come from the longer but safer north end of the trail.

Cedar Trail, red-blazed, connects the Northeast Trail with the Table Rocks Trail. Barely one mile long, this path is especially useful for designing interesting circular walks. Beginning where the Northeast Trail turns to climb Bonticou Ridge, the Cedar Trail descends to cross an old stone wall near a stream that once watered a small farm *(Figure 4-14)*. Rising through old fields grown to woodlands again, the trail soon reaches Cedar Drive, which it follows a short distance north (right). It briefly turns west (left), then leaves the old carriage road and descends along a path to end at the blue-blazed Table Rocks Trail.

Figure 4-14 Stone wall marking boundary of abandoned field on Cedar Trail west of Bonticou Crag.

THE AQUEDUCT

A great aqueduct was constructed at the beginning of the 20th century to supply New York City with water from reservoirs in the Catskill Mountains. Enroute from the Catskills, the aqueduct cuts through the Shawangunk ridges and emerges near the southeastern foot of Bonticou Crag *(Figure 4-15)*. From this point, some 500 feet above sea level, it snakes its way southward, very near the surface of the ground, following the eastern edge of the Shawangunks for several miles. The route of the aqueduct here looks rather like a raised railroad right-of-way. Although it has been used occasionally by walkers and bicyclists, it is *not* open to public use.

Figure 4-15 *Bonticou Crag seen from the Catskill Aqueduct.*

5. MOHONK

MOHONK

Mohonk Lake is the best known of the Shawangunk Sky Lakes. Barely $4/10$ mile long, it is one of the smallest (only Mud Pond is smaller) and – at 1,246 feet above sea level – the lowest in elevation. Geologically it is the most unusual of the Sky Lakes: The basin of Mohonk Lake lies in a gently-arched and "broken" anticline of the white conglomerate. The bottom of the lake has been eroded down to the underlying Ordovician shales which are exposed along the southeastern shore. The two sides of the arch are preserved as cliffs over the lake: Eagle Cliff Ridge to the southwest and the higher Sky Top Ridge, which forms the east side of the lake.

As the center of the original Smiley estates, Mohonk Lake became surrounded by a densely-developed network of carriage roads and footpaths, more complex than in any other region of the Shawangunks. Some of the short connecting paths will not be described in the following pages, but all are shown on the accompanying maps. For convenience here, the

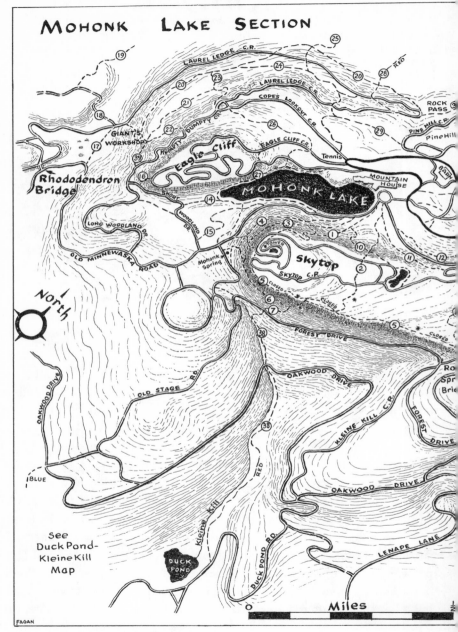

Figure 5-1 Map of the Mohonk Lake area.

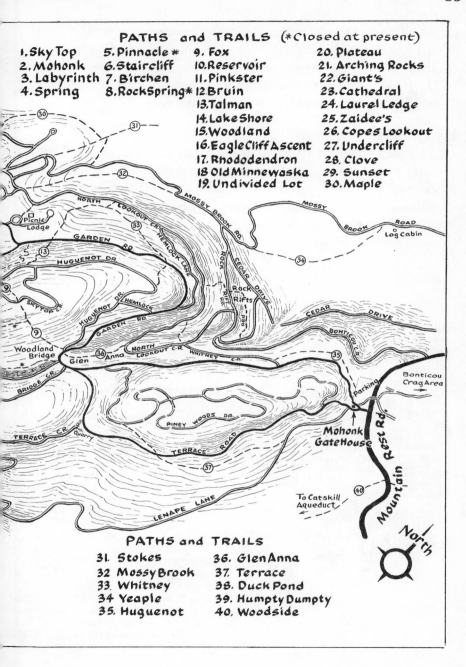

PATHS and TRAILS (*Closed at present)

1. Sky Top
2. Mohonk
3. Labyrinth
4. Spring

5. Pinnacle *
6. Staircliff
7. Birchen
8. RockSpring*

9. Fox
10. Reservoir
11. Pinkster
12. Bruin
13. Talman
14. Lake Shore
15. Woodland
16. Eagle Cliff Ascent
17. Rhododendron
18. Old Minnewaska
19. Undivided Lot

20. Plateau
21. Arching Rocks
22. Giant's
23. Cathedral
24. Laurel Ledge
25. Zaidee's
26. Copes Lookout
27. Undercliff
28. Clove
29. Sunset
30. Maple

PATHS and TRAILS

31. Stokes
32. Mossy Brook
33. Whitney
34. Yeaple
35. Huguenot

36. Glen Anna
37. Terrace
38. Duck Pond
39. Humpty Dumpty
40. Woodside

many walking routes will be divided into five sections. The northern limit of the Mohonk area is Mountain Rest Road, where all visitors (other than Mohonk Preserve members or passholders) must enter via the Gatehouse and its parking area. The southern limit is Rhododendron Bridge, about 2¼ miles southwest of the Gatehouse *(see map: Figure 5-1)*.

HISTORY

Mohonk Mountain House is the last of the great mountain resorts. It was constructed between 1879 and 1912. Sited at the north end of the lake, it is an extraordinary composite of stone and wooden structures, replete with gables, balconies and towers *(Figure 5-2)*. Radiating out from the building and the lake are miles of roads constructed between the 1870s and 1920s for horses and carriages. They were built on a base of stone rubble and covered with quarried shale fragments or cut directly into shale bedrock where it was at the surface. With well-planned drainage via

Figure 5-2 *Mohonk Mountain House (partial view). Blocks and outcrops of conglomerate rock have been incorporated into a maze of paths along the lakeshore.*

parallel ditches and culverts, these roads required a minimum of maintenance then and now. Yet they were constructed for as little as $1.00 a linear foot.

Figure 5-3
Summerhouse
near Mohonk
Mountain
House.

Along the carriage roads of the Mohonk area are many small gazebo-like structures located along cliff edges and at every appealing view. Most of these charming structures, called summerhouses by the Smileys, originated in the 19th century *(Figure 5-3)*. They were construct-ed of rustic wood and had thatched – later cedar-shingle – roofs. At one time there were over 200 of them on the Smiley estates. The Mountain House has preserved or renewed most of those on their current property, but the remainder, with very few exceptions, have disappeared. Hikers pausing at viewpoints on Mohonk Preserve or Minnewaska State Park lands may notice stubs of iron posts, driven into the rock, that supported the framework of former gazebos.

ACCESS

Long ago, most walkers in the Mohonk area were guests staying at the Mountain House. Today, many are day visitors who enter by way of the Gatehouse on Mountain Rest Road, parking at the Gatehouse and walking in or taking a seasonally-available shuttle bus to the Picnic Lodge day visitor center. All visitors, except for Mohonk Preserve members or passholders, are required to pay a guest fee to the Mountain House. (During peak periods, such as weekends during the fall foliage season, visitor parking areas may be filled to capacity early in the day.)

From the Gatehouse, walkers usually follow the recently-cut Huguenot Path to Whitney Carriage Road, which descends onto North Lookout Carriage Road. Following signs and using North Lookout Road, the walker can reach the Picnic Lodge, which is about one and one-half miles from the Gatehouse. This building provides restrooms and snacks, and is open daily during the summer months (it is open during the spring and fall on weekends only). The Picnic Lodge is a short distance from the north end of Mohonk Lake, where the visitor may choose from a number of branching carriage roads and footpaths *(see map: Figure 5-4)*. Please note that day visitors are not permitted to swim in the lake or to use the hotel or lakeside facilities.

LAKE AREA

Lake Shore Carriage Road was the earliest carriage road at Mohonk. Built in 1870, the first summer that the Smileys opened their inn to friends and guests, it is still the principal route along the east side of the lake.

Figure 5-5 *View southward from Eagle Cliff.*
The prominent cliff line is the Trapps. Millbrook Mountain is in the far distance.

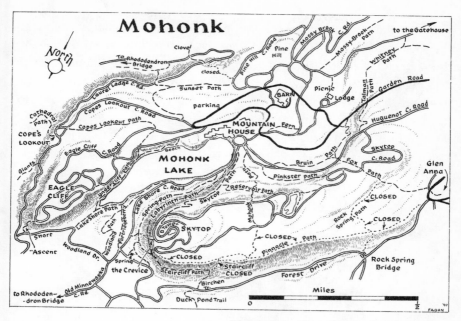

Figure 5-4 *Map of Mohonk Lake vicinity.*

Beginning at the north end of Mohonk Lake, it first follows the water's edge. Lake views and gazebos abound, and cliffs soar above, as **Labyrinth Path** begins on the left. Soon **Spring Path** branches to the left, offering a fine, nearly level route along the base of the cliffs. Then **Lake Shore Path** forks right from the carriage road, passing an old lean-to structure and continuing along the lake edge. The carriage road veers away from the lake through a pleasant wood and reaches an intersection with Forest Drive. Ahead, Lake Shore Road becomes **Old Minnewaska Road,** an early route to Lake Minnewaska. This carriage road curves down through hilly, forested terrain, soon passing Short and Long Woodland Drives, and eventually reaches Rhododendron Bridge about 1 ½ miles from the north end of the lake and 300 feet lower in elevation. **Short Woodland Drive** brings the walker close to the base of Eagle Cliff. There, just before the beginning of the Humpty Dumpty Carriage Road, is the **Eagle Cliff Ascent,** a challenging scramble up talus boulders and ledges to the magnificent southward view from Artists' Point atop Eagle Cliff *(Figure 5-5).*

Figure 5-6 *The Great Crevice in Sky Top Ridge. A challenging route connects the top of the ridge near the tower to the Labyrinth Path below.*

A pleasant walk can be made by taking Lake Shore Path, mentioned above, following the water's edge to the south end of the lake and continuing on **Undercliff Path.** The latter is a fairly level route that follows the water's edge until it reaches the swimming area. There, it rises to meet **Eagle Cliff Carriage Road,** where it ends. Another walking route off Lake Shore Carriage Road is **Spring Path.** This inviting, level route passes through abundant mountain laurel to reach the Mohonk Spring House. The spring was a stopping place for early visitors traveling by horse-drawn carriage to the Mountain House. For most, this was the last leg of a journey that had included travel by riverboat, ferry and/or rail to New Paltz. The Spring House was built in 1904. Although the spring still flows, the water is not safe for drinking.

Near the spring, spare, red-painted blazes on talus boulders indicate the very difficult **Labyrinth Path** scrambling toward the Sky Top cliffs and the base of the Great Crevice *(Figure 5-6)*. The Crevice is widely known as a strenuous route to Sky Top Tower. Climbing over the great conglomerate boulders into the dark, cave-like Crevice, one encounters a series of wooden ladders in the vertical-walled passage. The ladders lead up the ever-narrowing crevice and finally out into daylight. Here, the climber is on a broad ledge with views to the south, about 40 feet below Sky Top Tower. (To avoid congestion and delay, visitors are required to enter from below and to climb up only.)

SKY TOP RIDGE

Sky Top is the highly visible ridge (once called Paltz Point) that rises some 300 feet above Mohonk Lake. Seen from the lakeshore, its cliffs soar above massive talus boulders. These white ramparts and their boulder apron surround Sky Top on three sides. Built in 1923, Sky Top Tower (formally known as the Albert K. Smiley Memorial Tower) marks the highest point on the ridge and is visible for many miles around *(Figure 5-7)*. To reach it from the lake area, walkers have a choice of several routes.

The horse-drawn carriage route to Sky Top was the **Sky Top Carriage Road.** This road was rebuilt a number of times; the present road dates to 1895. Its extremely low gradient is achieved by dozens of curves and switchbacks. On the upper part of the ridge, Sky Top Road

Figure 5-7 *Sky Top Ridge and the Albert K. Smiley Memorial Tower seen from the east.*

had one-way-up and one-way-down segments, so that carriages did not have to be turned around at the top. A complete round trip from its beginning at Huguenot Drive is approximately four miles. Today, few walkers follow the long and twisting carriage road up to the tower (although this road is much used by cross-country skiers in the winter). Rather, they select one of several paths that ascend the slopes more steeply. **Sky Top Path** is the most direct route from the lake to Sky Top Tower. This well-worn foot-path begins near the Council House located at the beginning of Lake Shore Road. It rises steadily, switching back to lessen the steepness, passing fine views down onto the lake. Cutting across one loop of the carriage road, it reaches a higher curve of the road near the base of the tower. A stairway inside the tower brings the visitor to the observation deck, with its excellent views of the surrounding countryside. Both the high Catskills, 30 miles to the north, and the Hudson Highlands, 50 miles to the south, may be seen.

Figure 5-8
The Albert K. Smiley Memorial Tower atop Sky Top Ridge.

At the base of the tower is the hollow from which some of the building blocks were quarried. The pond now serves as a water reservoir for fire emergencies. This stone tower is the third structure to be built on this location *(Figure 5-8)*. The previous two, built in 1872 and 1878, were made of wood and burned down. Another reservoir, larger and pleasantly landscaped, is located along the Sky Top Carriage Road midway between Huguenot Drive and the tower; it provides water to the Mountain House gardens and can also be reached from Sky Top Path via the Reservoir Path.

An especially useful footpath called **Mohonk Path** begins in the vicinity of the Mountain House, rises onto the ridge, cuts across Reservoir Path and reaches the carriage road. It formerly continued by descending gently to Pinnacle Rock, a viewpoint at the southeast edge of Sky Top Ridge, but this section of the path has recently been closed by Mohonk Mountain House, and is no longer maintained *(Figure 5-9)*. The Mountain

Figure 5-9
Pinnacle Rock.
This rock formation is located along a path that is now closed for safety reasons.

House has also closed the northern end of Staircliff Path, a combination of ledges and wooden stairs that leads down the cliff face and along the base of the cliffs toward Mohonk Spring. A section which remains open to hikers leads to the red-marked Birchen Trail, a short spur that descends over talus boulders to Forest Drive.

Another useful footpath that cuts across Sky Top Ridge is **Fox Path,** which crosses the ridge near its lower northern end, from Huguenot Drive, heading to Woodland Bridge and Glen Anna. En route, it intersects Rock Spring Path. This route

Figure 5-10 The cliffs around Sky Top Ridge offer a great variety of scenic rockfalls, overhanging caves and fern-covered boulders.

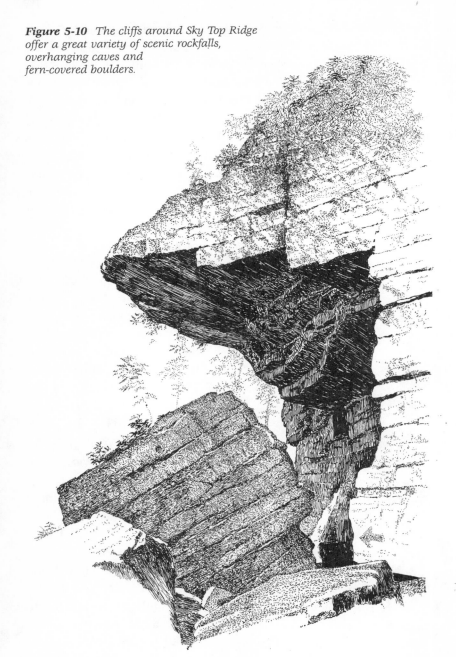

– which has also been closed recently by Mohonk Mountain House – leads over ledges, under fallen rock slabs and along the base of cliffs to cross Pinnacle Path and finally reach Rock Spring Bridge at the intersection of Kleine Kill Carriage Road and Forest Drive. We can only hope that the closure of this and other beautiful trails in this area will not be permanent *(Figure 5-10)*.

Figure 5-11 *Remnant of the past: horse and carriage still being used for excursions at the Mohonk Mountain House.*

EAGLE CLIFF

Across Mohonk Lake from Sky Top is another ridge, about 100 feet lower, called Eagle Cliff. The east side of this ridge is the dramatic scarp that rises above Mohonk Lake and Undercliff Path. At the south end of the ridge, this cliff line curves sharply to the west and northwest. Because of the complex faults that slice through this section of the mountains, the west slope of Eagle Cliff has a multi-tiered relief, with alternating zones of dipping strata, talus blocks and cliffs.

The crest of the ridge is reached via the **Eagle Cliff Carriage Road.** This road, which starts near the Mountain House, maintains a gentle gradient by following a very sinuous course. Like Sky Top Road, Eagle Cliff Road had a one-way loop course to avoid the need for carriages to pass each other *(Figure 5-11)*. At almost every viewpoint along the road stands one of the rustic summerhouses, all well-situated to afford carriage riders – and now walkers – the best panoramas of Mohonk Lake and the Sky Top cliffs across the lake *(Figure 5-12)*.

Figure 5-12 *Summerhouse along Eagle Cliff Carriage Road.*

The old carriage road makes a fine walk. A number of bits of trail that cut off loops of the road provide short cuts, usually along cliff edges. So it is possible to reach the most superb views, near the south end of Eagle Cliff, in under ¾ mile from the Mountain House (one way). The entire length of this meandering road is about 2½ miles.

Near the south end of Eagle Cliff, several summerhouses perch on ledges, with outstanding views toward the Trapps cliffs. Near one of these is a flight of wooden steps, the top of the

Figure 5-13
Along Humpty Dumpty
Carriage Road,
looking up at a
summerhouse on
Eagle Cliff.

Eagle Cliff Ascent. At the bottom of the rough, rocky trail is a carriage road called Short Woodland Drive. Slightly to the west (right) is a three-way intersection with **Humpty Dumpty Carriage Road** and Long Woodland Drive. Humpty Dumpty Road *(Figure 5-13)* winds its way through a terrain of massive, fallen boulders and past good viewpoints to arrive at Copes Lookout, one of the many fine vistas of Mohonk. The lookout may also be reached by either the **Copes Lookout Carriage Road** or **Copes Lookout Path,** both starting near the Mountain House.

Once at the Lookout, the walker has a number of choices for further exploration of this western slope. An easy route down is to follow **Laurel Ledge Carriage Road.** This excellent shale road starts at Copes Lookout and angles down a dense, forested slope. Following a steep dropoff, the road soon reaches a sharp bend. This is Rock Pass, with the blue-blazed Maple Path branching northward, and the red-blazed Plateau Path leading down to the west. Further along, the carriage road passes the steeply descending **Clove Path** (red), and soon reaches the yellow trail descending to Zaidee's Bower. This trail is actually a circular rock scramble down a steep hemlock-covered slope to some secluded rock outcrops. Soon the carriage road again intersects the red-blazed Plateau Path, and finally Laurel Ledge Road ends

Figure 5-14
Entering the
Giant's Workshop
via the Giant's Path.
These crevices
are located uphill
from Laurel Ledge
Carriage Road near
its intersection
with the Old
Minnewaska
Trail.

at Rhododendron Bridge – about two miles from Copes Lookout. (The trails beyond this point are described in the next chapter.)

From the Copes Lookout-Humpty Dumpty Road area, there are a number of additional trails that lead downslope and may be used to explore the rugged terrain between that elevation and the lower segment of Laurel Ledge Road 200 feet below. (It should be noted that the area below the level of Humpty Dumpty Road is part of the Mohonk Preserve.) These trails are, for the most part, steep and challenging routes for the physically fit with good footgear. One of these is **Giant's Path,** a blue-blazed trail that leads from Humpty Dumpty Road down into the Giant's Workshop, a chaotic maze of crevices and fallen slabs *(Figure 5-14)*. Another is **Cathedral Path,** a blue-blazed trail that starts on the scenic ledge at Copes Lookout, which features a larger-than-usual gazebo. Overlooking it is a bronze plaque that commemorates the founding of the Mohonk Trust (now the Mohonk Preserve). Near this gazebo, the Cathedral Path *(Figure 5-15)* drops sharply down over ledges and winds among talus boulders until it ends at Plateau Path, just above Laurel Ledge Road.

Figure 5-15 *Cathedral Path.*

An especially intriguing trail intersects the Cathedral Path just below the initial dropoff from Copes. This is **Arching Rocks Path,** a red-blazed trail that follows the base of overhanging cliffs southward to intersect the blue-blazed Giant's Path. By following the latter trail to the right, the hiker soon reaches an intersection with Plateau Path. Next is a flat ledge with good views and, just beyond, the Giant's Path begins its tortuous descent through the Giant's Workshop.

GLEN ANNA AND NORTH LOOKOUT SLOPE

A look at a topographic map of the Mohonk region shows a well-defined notch cutting across the ridges half a mile northeast of the lake. This notch is formed by the valley of the Kleine Kill flowing south, and a

Figure 5-16
Hemlock trees in
Rock Rift area growing
on the edge of crevices
which form along joint cracks.
These trees have developed a
cantilevered root support system.

north-flowing stream which has cut the valley called Glen Anna. The divide between the two valleys is called Woodland Bridge. This divide marks the location of one of the many north-trending faults that cut across the Shawangunks. The double-headed valley results in a roughly congruent bending of the many carriage roads found between the Gatehouse and the Lake areas. In Glen Anna, the roads curve and intersect in so complex a manner that one needs to follow the map closely here.

Most walkers coming in from the Gatehouse parking area will be walking on **North Lookout Carriage Road,** which may be followed around the contours of Glen Anna to the Picnic Lodge and Mohonk Lake. A short distance beyond Glen Anna, fine views begin to appear, and the reason for the name of the North Lookout becomes clear.

Walkers who follow the lower section of North Lookout Carriage Road northward (to the right) from its intersection with Whitney Road will be descending along the Glen Anna stream toward the intriguing Rock Rift area *(Figure 5-16).* A quarter mile from Whitney Road, North Lookout Road ends at a three-way intersection. To the right is Bonticou Carriage Road, which leads through fine hemlock groves, crosses Mohonk Road in three-fourths of a mile, and continues toward the Bonticou Crag region (see previous section). To the left, the **Rock Rift Carriage Road** leads past the Rock Rift Trail and ends at Cedar Drive. A left on Cedar Drive leads in a short distance to

Figure 5-17
Crevice in Rock Rift.

Mossy Brook Road; to the right, Cedar Drive leads northeast toward the Crag region but is interrupted where the Glen Anna stream washed out a bridge crossing decades ago.

The Rock Rifts are a group of deep crevices formed by the slow widening of joint cracks that cut down into a broad conglomerate surface

located at the end of North Lookout Road *(Figure 5-17)*. The crevices may be entered by following Rock Rift Road to the left from North Lookout Road and soon turning right onto the outcrop surface and down into the first wide crevice *(Figure 5-18)*. Here a red-blazed trail leads through a complex labyrinth of canyon-like clefts and collapsed slab-caves where hemlocks have adapted to the crevices and narrow passages in various picturesque ways *(Figure 5-19)*.

At the bottom of Rock Rift crevices, the trail emerges from the cliffs and leads out onto **Old Glen Anna Road.** To the right, this road ascends to join Bonticou Road; to the left, it descends to intersect Cedar Drive. A short

Figure 5-18 Rock Rift. This hemlock, growing from the bottom of one of the intersecting crevices of the Rift area, has nearly blocked the passage.

Figure 5-19
*Hemlock tree
growing along the
Rock Rift crevices.
The irregular sur-
face and restricted
sunlight have
resulted in the
peculiar curved
shape of the tree.*

distance west of
the intersection,
Cedar Drive meets
the lower end of
Rock Rift Road
before ending
at **Mossy Brook Carriage Road.** The lower part of Mossy Brook
Road is not much used today by walkers because it ends far down on
Mohonk Road where no parking is available. But half a mile in from
Mohonk Road is the Log Cabin. This interesting old building, made of
notched oak and chestnut logs, was home to generations of the Yeaple
family. Its exact age is unknown, but the style of its construction is typical
of 200 years ago, and it is certainly the oldest building on Mountain House
lands *(Figure 5-20)*. The upper reaches of Mossy Brook Road cut back

and forth across the
stream for which it is
named, making an inter-
esting route between the
Rock Rift-Glen Anna
region and the Rock
Pass-Pine Hill region
near Mohonk Lake.

Figure 5-20
*The Log Cabin along
Mossy Brook Carriage Road.*

DUCK POND – KLEINE KILL

From Woodland and Rock Spring Bridges, the stream called Kleine Kill cuts out a valley which deepens to the south. Crossing under Forest and Oakwood Drives, the Kill feeds into Duck Pond. This region may be described as the slope below the eastern cliffs of Sky Top Ridge and

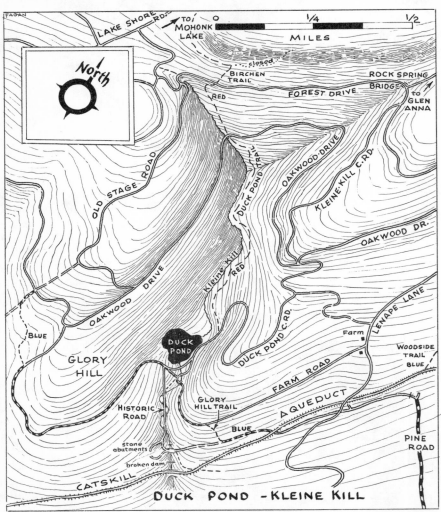

Figure 5-21 *Detail map of Duck Pond-Kleine Kill area.*

above the Catskill Aqueduct. An area entirely of Ordovician shale, it is atypical of the Shawangunks because of its lack of cliffs and pitch pines. It is nonetheless a fine area for long walks in deep woods *(see map: Figure 5-21).*

The northwestern edge of this area is **Forest Drive,** which may be reached from Lake Shore Carriage Road near Mohonk Spring. Forest Drive was built in 1882 during a period when the carriage routes were being greatly expanded to include new properties that Albert Smiley was adding to Mohonk. Forest Drive follows the contours of the landscape to end at Oakwood Drive near Lenape Lane about 1½ miles from Lake Shore Road. It provides pleasant walking as it follows the base of the talus blocks fallen from the cliffs high above.

Oakwood Drive is one of the longest carriage roads built by the Smileys. Following a near-level course below and parallel to Forest Drive as it cuts across Kleine Kill, Oakwood Drive rises westward out of the

Figure 5-22
Along Duck Pond
Carriage Road. A white oak
provides shade amidst the
hay fields that border this
old, winding road.

valley and climbs the slopes of Glory Hill. Above Glory Hill, it enters the forest and offers the walker another mile of varied landscape and gentle grades on its way to Rhododendron Bridge.

Duck Pond, formed in 1908 by damming the Kleine Kill, is a pleasant destination. At 600 feet in elevation, it is well below the level of Oakwood Drive. The pond may be reached from the higher slopes by following **Duck Pond Carriage Road** down a meandering course from the intersection of Oakwood Drive and Kleine Kill Carriage Road *(Figure 5-22)*. This junction is confusing because the three different carriage roads angle off in four directions. **Kleine Kill Carriage Road** runs from this intersection to Rock Spring Bridge, three-fourths of a mile away.

The pond may also be reached by following the red-blazed **Duck Pond Trail** downslope from Forest Drive. The trail starts beside a gazebo across the road from the Birchen Trail. It follows a tributary of Kleine Kill downslope past shale outcrops. Crossing Oakwood Drive, the trail descends steeply for another three-fourths of a mile before reaching Duck Pond Road just uphill from the pond itself *(Figure 5-23)*.

Figure 5-23 *Duck Pond, with Sky Top in the background.*

Figure 5-24 A bridge over Kleine Kill on the historic
old road downstream from Duck Pond.

The blue-blazed **Glory Hill Trail** starts at the intersection of an old road with the Catskill Aqueduct *(see Figure 5-21)* and may be reached from an unofficial parking area at the end of Pine Road (which extends north from Butterville Road). To reach the trail from this parking area, go past a chain and follow the dirt road which roughly parallels the Aqueduct, located just uphill. (It should be noted that entry from Pine Hill Road requires crossing lands owned by the Mohonk Mountain House, and a valid permit must be obtained.) The Glory Hill Trail may also be reached from Duck Pond and Oakwood Drive, as shown on Figure 5-21.

This dirt road soon crosses Lenape Lane and then cuts across the Aqueduct at an acute angle. Here the blue trail begins. It follows the road for a short distance, then turns left, leaving the road, and heads uphill. The old road continues ahead for about ¼ mile to a bridge over the Kleine Kill and to the historic wagon road that follows the stream northward *(Figure 5-24)*. Here are a series of broken dams, interesting old bridges and stone abutments.

After leaving the old road, the blue-blazed Glory Hill Trail continues uphill, and soon turns left on an old farm road. In about ⅓ mile, the road crosses the outlet of Duck Pond, and the blue blazes lead the hiker up a left fork and then left again on another dirt farm road, with the pond a short distance to the north. The blue-blazed trail continues along the road as it curves south, west and then north, trending gently upward past the open fields of Glory Hill. About 2/3 mile from the pond, the blue trail leaves the road, cuts through the woods and intersects a faint road. The trail follows this road uphill a short distance to reach Oakwood Drive, where the blazes end.

To the right, Oakwood Drive provides a level route to the Kleine Kill, where the red-blazed Duck Pond Trail leads down to Duck Pond. Alternatively, the hiker can cross Oakwood Drive and continue straight ahead uphill along the faint road for a short distance to reach another, better-preserved road (Old Stage Road) at a sharp curve. Ahead to the left this road gradually rises to reach Forest Drive near the upper reaches of the Kleine Kill and just west of the northern end of the Duck Pond Trail.

Another blue-blazed route, the **Woodside Trail,** begins at the Catskill Aqueduct about ¼ mile north of Lenape Lane and leads uphill approximately two miles to Mountain Rest Road near the Gatehouse. It should be borne in mind that, for most of its length, the Aqueduct itself is closed to public use.

6. TRAPPS-
PETER'S KILL

The Trapps is a prominent, two-mile-long section of the east-facing cliff scarp of the Shawangunks. The southern edge of the Trapps rises dramatically over Route 44-55. At its northern end, near Rhododendron Bridge, the cliff declines in height and ends in the fault zone at the base of Eagle Cliff. In between, the cliff face reaches as high as 300 feet. To the west, paralleling the Trapps, is the long uplift that includes the multiple knobs of Dickie Barre, Ronde Barre and Rock Hill and the cliffs of Lost City. Between this rise and the Trapps is the valley of the Coxing Kill, called the Clove. West of the Dickie Barre-Rock Hill ridge is the valley of the Peter's Kill *(see map: Figure 6-1)*.

The Trapps cliffs, when seen from New Paltz or from Route 299 west of the Wallkill River, appear as a straight and undeviating cliff line. But closer examination of the topographic map shows a distinct offset caused by cross-cutting faults. A notch near this fault zone has provided a route across this formidable ridge, probably since the last Ice Age. The modern Route 44-55 uses this notch today (somewhat deepened by blasting).

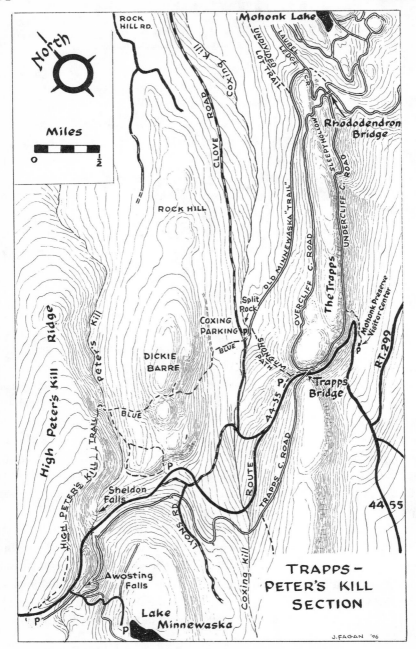

Figure 6-1 *Map of Trapps-Peter's Kill section.*

The two streams that flow between the Trapps and the High Peter's Kill ridge – the Coxing Kill and the Peter's Kill – are nearly parallel and only about a mile apart, but they have different origins. The Coxing Kill, in part the outlet of Lake Minnewaska, drains the area between that lake and Millbrook Mountain. The Peter's Kill, although it passes near Lake Minnewaska, is actually the outlet of the more distant Lake Awosting; its watershed is the region surrounding Lake Awosting and extending to the northeast. Both of these streams flow over exposed conglomerate bedrock, often stained yellow-brown with organic matter carried by the water. Rapids and small waterfalls form where the water races over ledges. Deeper pools, shaded by hemlock, make cool havens in the summer.

The direction of the ridges and stream valleys in the Shawangunks is controlled primarily by folding and, to some extent, by faulting. The basic structure consists of northeast-plunging folds of the conglomerate formation, in places cut by north and northwest-trending faults. The

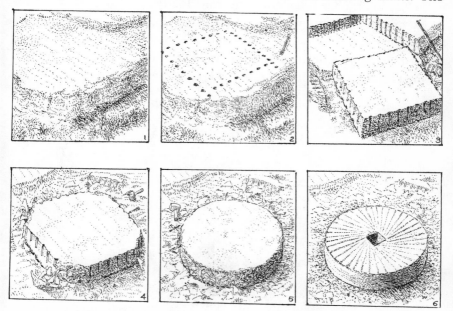

Figure 6-2 *The various stages of cutting a millstone: 1 through 6. 1: Starting with a conglomerate layer of proper thickness. 2: Outlining a square with hand-drilled holes. 3: Removal of a square block after splitting the rock by use of wedges. 4 and 5: Chiseling the edges to form a circular shape. 6: A completed millstone.*

Clove of the Coxing Kill is primarily a syncline (downfold) of conglomerate layers, complicated by faults that cut across the western side of the valley near Lost City and Dickie Barre. The ridge between the Coxing Kill and the Peter's Kill is essentially a northeast-plunging anticline, though it too is cut across by faults.

HISTORY

By the early 20th century, the Smiley family holdings had been extended to include the Trapps cliffs. Carriage roads had been constructed past the cliffs to connect the Mohonk and Minnewaska resorts. The Smileys' mountain hotels provided new employment opportunities for some of the local subsistence farmers. But long before the Smileys arrived, the inhabitants had used the natural resources of the mountain by timbering for lumber and for charcoal and by cutting millstones from the hard, white conglomerate bedrock

The millstones ranged in size from 1½ feet to 7 feet in diameter. Made by the slow process of hand drilling and chiseling *(Figure 6-2)*, the Shawangunk millstones were valued for use in grinding wheat and corn in watermills. More millstones were quarried from Rock Hill than from anywhere else in the Shawangunks. In the Rock Hill area, numerous millstone

Figure 6-3 Remains of millstones found at Rock Hill. The one on the left is unfinished; the one on the right is completed but broken.

Your Invitation To Join The
NY-NJ TRAIL CONFERENCE
GPO Box 2250 ○ NY NY 10116

Hikers and friends who wish to support the efforts of the Conference to maintain and protect 1,300 miles of marked foot trails in the NY/NJ area are invited to join as members. Dues include a subscription to our bi-monthly, The *Trail Walker*, 20-25% discounts on our publications (& 10% discounts at 20 local outdoor stores), and use of our extensive Library ...*and, above all, the opportunity to protect the hiking trails and to get involved!*

Name(s)_____

Address_____

City_____ State_____ Zip_____

Phone(s) Day _____/_____ Eve _____/_____

E-mail?_____ (Please PRINT clearly)

Check ✓...	Individual	Joint/Family
Regular	☐ $21	☐ $26
Sponsor	☐ $45	☐ $50
Benefactor	☐ $95	☐ $100
Student	☐ $15	☐ $20
Senior	☐ $15	☐ $20
Ltd. Income	☐ $15	☐ $20
Life	☐ $400	☐ $600 (2 adults)

Do you belong to a hiking or outdoor club(s)? If yes, please list:

_____

☐ Mailing: Check box to left if you do *__not__* want your name exchanged with others (hiking clubs, etc.)

☐ *Check Here for the NEW MEMBER SPECIAL*: Join before 12/31/99 and take $2 off any of the above dues rates.

Hiking Maps & Guides...

...By the People Who Maintain the Trails...

Map Sets

HARRIMAN-BEAR MOUNTAIN TRAILS / 2 maps
EAST HUDSON TRAILS / 3 maps
WEST HUDSON TRAILS / 2 maps
CATSKILL TRAILS / 5 maps
SHAWANGUNK TRAILS / 4 maps
NORTH JERSEY TRAILS / 2 maps
SOUTH TACONIC TRAILS / 1 map
NORTH KITTATINNY TRAILS / 2 maps
SOUTH KITTATINNY TRAILS / 2 maps
PYRAMID MOUNTAIN TRAILS / 1 map
HUDSON PALISADES TRAILS / 2 maps
HIGH MOUNTAIN TRAILS / 1 map

Books & Guides

THE NEW YORK WALK BOOK
APPALACHIAN TRAIL GUIDE, NY/NJ
CIRCUIT HIKES IN NORTHERN NJ
GUIDE TO THE LONG PATH, NY/NJ
HEALTH HINTS FOR HIKERS
50 HIKES IN NEW JERSEY
50 HIKES IN THE HUDSON VALLEY
IRON MINE TRAILS: NJ/NY HIGHLANDS
BEST HIKES WITH CHILDREN: NJ
BEST HIKES W/CHILDREN: HUDSON-CATSKILL
HIGH PEAKS OF THE NORTHEAST (NY/VT/NH/ME)
HIKING THE CATSKILLS
HIKING THE DELAWARE WATER GAP NRA
HARRIMAN TRAILS: A GUIDE & HISTORY

Full catalog & order form included with membership or on request.
See address on reverse or call us anytime at 212/685-9699.
E-mail info requests: nynjtc@aol.com. Include postal address for reply.

quarries lie scattered along the low ridge *(Figure 6-3)*. It is not uncommon today to encounter stone boat tracks in the woods. These routes, made for millstone transport, are recognizable by their being wider than most foot trails but narrower and steeper than the carriage roads.

Millstones were quarried in the Shawangunks throughout the 19th century. Many were shipped via the Delaware and Hudson Canal, located just northwest of Rock Hill. When the Wallkill Valley Railroad was built in the 1870s, a wider market increased the output of millstones. Late in the 19th century, several hundred tons of millstones were taken out yearly. Rosendale, at the north end of the Shawangunks, became a principal shipping station.

Evidence of another early industry in the Shawangunks may be found along the Coxing Kill near the parking area on Clove Road. The waterfall at Split Rock *(Figure 6-4)* was the site of a sawmill which operated during the last century. Remnants of the foundations of the sawyer's buildings may be seen between the stream and the parking area.

Figure 6-4 *Falls and pool at Split Rock. Just upstream is a newly-rebuilt bridge where Old Minnewaska Trail crosses the Coxing Kill just beyond the Mohonk Preserve parking area on Clove Road.*

ACCESS

There are two principal points of access to this area: the parking
area on Route 44-55, just west of Trapps Bridge, and the one at Split Rock
on the Coxing Kill, located on Clove Road about one mile north of Route
44-55. Both parking areas are maintained by the Mohonk Preserve. The
roads and trails in this section are also within reasonable walking distance from Lake Mohonk, north of Rhododendron Bridge. The High
Peter's Kill Trail may be reached from the Awosting parking area near
the entrance to Minnewaska State Park Preserve.

Access from the Trapps offers a variety of walking, skiing and biking routes along trails and old carriage roads. The routes from the Coxing
Kill trailhead are footpaths only.

The most recent "industry" centered on the Shawangunk conglomerate – rock-climbing – is focused in this area *(Figure 6-5)*. The hard white
rock forms an ideal medium for this modern sport, and "the Gunks," as
they are called by climbers, are internationally famous *(Figure 6-6)*.
The Trapps cliffs, offering a great range of climbing routes and levels of
difficulty, have long been a magnet for climbers *(Figure 6-7)*. In 1996, the

Figure 6-5 *Top of a rock pinnacle at the newly-opened climbing area of the
Minnewaska State Park Preserve. This pinnacle was formed by the separation of
rock masses along joint crevices which developed at right angles to one another.*

Figure 6-6 Cliff face above Undercliff Carriage Road about one mile from Trapps Bridge.

Figure 6-7 A popular climbing area along Undercliff Carriage Road.

Minnewaska State Park Preserve opened a new area to rock climbers. The area designated for climbing is along the spectacular line of cliffs located near the former Minnewaska Ski Center on Route 44-55, west of Trapps Bridge and east of the main entrance to the Park Preserve. A parking area has been opened for climbers and hikers.

CARRIAGE ROADS

A very popular, relatively level walk is the circular combination of Undercliff and Overcliff Carriage Roads, starting at Trapps Bridge (*Figure 6-8*). Trapps Bridge is often used as a landmark for directions in this area. It is the only old carriage road bridge that has been rebuilt from wood to steel and it is, therefore, also referred to as "the steel bridge." It is reached from the far end of the recently constructed parking area on Route 44-55 by way of a new path that leads uphill to the stone stairway in the abutment of the bridge. Undercliff and Overcliff Carriage Roads

Figure 6-8 *The intersection of Overcliff and Undercliff Carriage Roads at Trapps Bridge.*

start at the triangular intersection on the north side of Trapps Bridge. From the bridge, Undercliff is the right fork, Overcliff the left.

Undercliff Carriage Road, which follows the base of the towering Trapps cliffs, is surely one of the finer walking routes of the Shawangunks. Completed by the Smileys in 1903, the road was built along the top of a mass of talus boulders fallen from the cliffs. Its construction involved enormous amounts of hand labor to remove or reposition great blocks of conglomerate, to break boulders into building

Figure 6-9
Undercliff
Carriage Road,
showing the
carefully con-
structed base of
conglomerate
blocks.

stones for support walls, and to add wagonloads of quarried shale *(Figure 6-9).* Finally, the present near-level road was achieved – ideal for touring by horse and carriage then, and no less ideal today for walking, skiing and bicycling.

To begin on Undercliff Road, take the right fork of the triangle, passing between two huge fallen boulders. The road soon crosses a shale outcrop and then approaches a great vertical cliff of conglomerate. The juxtaposition of the two rock types here is at a fault zone.

For the next 1½ miles, the carriage road follows the base of the line of cliffs, past huge fallen rock masses. Eastward views enliven the route. At intervals, short, steep yellow-marked scrambles lead up to popular climbing routes on the cliffs. The popularity of rock climbing has made this one of the most heavily used areas in the Shawangunks.

Nevertheless, Undercliff Road is a spectacular place and should not be missed *(Figure 6-10)*.

About 1.8 miles from Trapps Bridge, a wooded glen known as Sleepy Hollow lies ahead at the foot of the cliff. The carriage road veers away from the cliff line and continues through a gently sloping forest to reach an intersection that is 2½ miles from the start. This is Rhododendron Bridge. A map on the bridge helps to clarify this complex junction of old carriage roads. A circular hike back to Trapps Bridge may be made by curving left here (do not cross Rhododendron Bridge) onto Overcliff Road. It is a little over two miles back to Trapps Bridge via Overcliff.

While Undercliff is remarkable for its dramatic overhanging cliffs, **Overcliff Carriage Road** is noted for its views toward the west. From Rhododendron Bridge, Overcliff Road curves to the west, passing Sleepy Hollow on the left (south). It rises through a notch to reach the west side of the Trapps ridge. The shoulder of the road falls away sharply to allow an unimpeded panorama of the Catskills beyond the Rondout Valley – the first of many fine views along this road.

Figure 6-11 shows the relationship of the somewhat higher Overcliff Road on the northwest dipping (downward tilting) side of the Trapps ridge to the lower Undercliff Road on the opposite, cliff side of the ridge. Also

Figure 6-10 *Trapps cliffs above Undercliff Carriage Road.*

in contrast to Undercliff, the Overcliff side is relatively open and unshaded. For most of the route, the bare rock outcrops, dipping as steeply as 40 degrees, support little vegetation. Trees are mostly pitch pine and are sparse – all the better for viewpoints. For the last mile before reaching the Trapps, the views include the Lost City cliffs across the Clove (valley) and Dickie Barre. Finally, the views are lost as the road curves southward into denser woods before arriving at the triangle at Trapps Bridge.

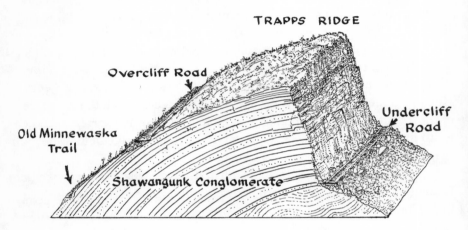

Figure 6-11 *This cutaway view of the Trapps ridge (looking north) illustrates the relative positions of Undercliff and Overcliff Carriage Roads and of Old Minnewaska Trail on the ridge.*

Laurel Ledge Carriage Road also starts at Rhododendron Bridge. Heading west from the bridge, the left fork is Overcliff Road; to the right, curving north, is Laurel Ledge. This lovely route turns past a wooded swamp through an area of living and fallen hemlocks, mountain laurel and rhododendrons. In less than half a mile from Rhododendron Bridge, Old Minnewaska Trail branches to the left (west). Then, almost immediately, Giant's Path (blue) can be seen on the right. Laurel Ledge Road continues northward, steadily rising on a long switchback, and eventually reaches the Mohonk Lake area in less than two miles from Rhododendron Bridge.

TRAILS

Old Minnewaska Trail is a carriage road built by the Smileys in 1879 to connect the Mohonk Mountain House with the newly acquired Minnewaska property. A few decades later, other routes replaced this one for carriage traffic between the two resorts. The original route was then poorly maintained and has so narrowed in places that calling it a trail now seems quite suitable. A portion of the old road is marked with blue blazes.

The lower, western end of Old Minnewaska Trail is reached from the Coxing Kill parking area on Clove Road. The carriage road crosses this stream on a newly rebuilt bridge.

The blue-blazed trail begins at the Coxing Kill and heads uphill, immediately passing the red-blazed Shongum Path on the right (south). This end of the old road is wide and eroded. The north-facing slope is heavily wooded; hemlocks are especially abundant. In about half a mile, a deep cut in the road is reached. A small stream here was once crossed by a bridge. The bridge abutments of shaped conglomerate blocks may still be seen. After this stream crossing, the roadway begins to narrow, the result of tree growth and the long absence of wheeled traffic. A little farther along, a faint track to the left leads to a stone quarry, long abandoned but still containing large, beautifully cut blocks of conglomerate *(Figure 6-12)*. The hand-cut drill holes that edge the blocks still seem fresh. Farther uphill along Old Minnewaska Trail lies a single stone

Figure 6-12 *Abandoned stone quarry near Old Minnewaska Trail.*

Figure 6-13 *Along the High Peter's Kill Trail. The trail runs through this gap in the outcrop and has worn down to the bedrock in the foreground.*

block, perhaps fallen from a Mohonk-bound wagon a hundred years ago.

About 1.8 miles from the Coxing Kill and 300 feet higher in elevation, the trail reaches an intersection with the Undivided Lot Trail. This blue-blazed footpath leads north to Clove Chapel (see Bonticou section). The Old Minnewaska Trail, now unmarked, continues to the right (east).

The upper part of the trail has a number of good views towards Rock Hill and beyond to the Catskills. At one viewpoint, several of Mohonk's gazebos may be seen along Eagle Cliff to the northeast. Finally, the trail turns through several short curves and reaches the Laurel Ledge Carriage Road. This point is a little less than 2½ miles from the parking area at Coxing Kill and less than half a mile from Rhododendron Bridge.

Shongum Path is a segment of a centuries-old Indian trail that cuts across the ridge at the Trapps notch. It now serves as a connection between Trapps Bridge and the Coxing Kill trailhead. Marked with red blazes, the trail starts about mid-point on the short path (unmarked) that connects the new parking area on Route 44-55 with Trapps Bridge itself. From the Trapps Bridge area, the trail descends over steeply-sloping bedrock and through a dense stand of hemlocks. After losing about 300 feet in elevation, the trail levels off. Nearing an old stone wall, the hiker may be able to hear the Coxing Kill below. The Shongum Path ends at the Old Minnewaska Trail just across the Coxing Kill from the parking area on Clove Road. The total length is approximately half a mile.

High Peter's Kill Trail is one of the finest, most varied trails in the Shawangunks *(Figure 6-13)*. It is 3½ miles long and relatively strenuous, depending partly on the direction it is taken. The trail is marked with blue blazes and runs approximately east to west from the Coxing Kill parking area to Route 44-55 near the entrance to Minnewaska State Park Preserve.

At its eastern end, the trail begins across Clove Road from the parking area. This area was once farmed, and the land is still marked by numerous low stone walls. A wet section is traversed on narrow boardwalks, with sphagnum moss growing below the planks. In a pleasant stand of hemlocks, a small stream is crossed. About a third of a mile from the start, the blue trail, which has been following an eroded woods road, turns sharply left to parallel a massive old stone wall *(Figure 6-14)*. The woods road it leaves behind ascends to the northeast; it soon encounters some well-worn, unmarked paths that head up the mountain toward an

Figure 6-14 Stone wall along the High Peter's Kill Trail near its eastern end. This wall served to divide old pasture lands located at the foot of Dickie Barre.

Figure 6-15 *Cliffs at Lost City. This is the eastern edge of an area of vertical walls and fissures frequented by rock climbers, about half a mile northwest of the Coxing Kill parking area.*

impressive line of cliffs used by rock climbers. This is Lost City, a fault-
ed section of Coxing Clove, which has canyon-like fissures in the towering conglomerate outcrops *(Figure 6-15)*.

The High Peter's Kill Trail, however, follows a level course to the
west, past more stone walls and over the outlet of an old, improved
spring. Just beyond another stream, the trail begins to ascend, in places
following a cleared route known as the Dugway, which was once used for
moving millstones. Passing lichen-encrusted outcrops, the trail climbs
more steeply. As it nears the crest of the ridge, a side trail leads to the
right (north). A short distance along this side trail, there is a good view
back toward the Clove and to the Trapps beyond. Ahead, the High Peter's
Kill Trail rises to a pass between the low cliffs of Dickie Barre. The elevation here is 1,270 feet above sea level, about 600 feet higher than the
starting point of the trail.

From the crest, the blue blazes lead the walker through the woods to
the west side of Dickie Barre. An open area is reached where the smooth-
ly glaciated bedrock is covered with striations and chattermarks. A few
dozen yards off the trail, there is a dramatic view into the clove of the
Peter's Kill. The roar of rapids far below can be heard. From these ledges,
the blue blazes lead down through dense mountain laurel to the Peter's
Kill. Wooden bridges cross the main stream and the secondary channel.

The Peter's Kill is a lovely mountain stream with rapidly flowing
water cascading over mossy ledges and swirling into pools. The nature of
the stream here is controlled by the bedrock itself. The water follows the
dipping strata, rebounds from joint-bounded outcrops and drops over
thicker conglomerate ledges. By following a faint path upstream along the
Peter's Kill, the hiker may reach the old downhill ski area. Developed in
the 1960s by the Minnewaska resort, "Ski-Minne" was closed in 1976.
Further upstream along the Peter's Kill is Sheldon Falls, well worth a visit.

From the footbridges, the blue-marked Peter's Kill Trail climbs the
west side of the valley, ascending the High Peter's Kill cliffs. After a climb
of several hundred feet, a more gradual rise brings the walker to a clifftop
route with more good views. Back to the east are the former downhill ski
runs, with the cliffs of Dickie Barre above them. Below lies Sheldon Falls
(Figure 6-16). The falls may only be heard from here, but the ruins of a

hydroelectric plant are visible *(Figure 6-17)*. This structure, built of blocks of conglomerate in 1924, provided electricity for the two Minnewaska hotels located on the mountain top, about one mile away.

Figure 6-16   *Sheldon Falls on the Peter's Kill.*

Figure 6-17 *Ruins of old stone powerhouse near Sheldon Falls on the Peter's Kill.*

Across open ledges, the trail continues to rise rather gradually for another quarter of a mile, then levels off and descends slightly. Nearing the west terminus, the trail is once again in dense woods and mountain laurel. The blue blazes lead to Route 44-55. Just across the road is the Minnewaska hikers' parking area, also called the Awosting parking area.

It is possible to return to the Coxing Kill from this end of the High Peter's Kill Trail by using the Trapps Carriage Road. From the hikers' parking area, follow the level dirt road east for a quarter of a mile to the Minnewaska entrance road. Across the automobile bridge, the Trapps Carriage Road turns left into the woods along the stream and loops down past Awosting Falls. The carriage road arrives at Trapps Bridge in 3¼ miles. From there, the Shongum Path leads down to the Coxing Kill parking area.

In 1996, several new trails were laid out in the vicinity of the newly-opened Minnewaska State Park Preserve parking area on Route 44-55. Most of these trails lead to the rock climbing areas or connect various climbing routes along the clifftops, and will be open only to those with climbing permits. For hikers, a trail is being built from the parking area to the Peter's Kill.

From the parking area, this trail proceeds west through a broad meadow, enters the woods near some rock outcrops, and begins a gradual descent towards the Peter's Kill. Here the trail runs along an often-slippery, pavement-like surface formed by the dipping conglomerate beds. Reaching the stream at a lovely cascade and pool, the trail proceeds downstream along the rushing waters *(Figure 6-18)*. Soon, at an open area, the route divides. The hiker has the choice of turning right, uphill, and returning to the parking area, or continuing ahead, following the stream. The trail ahead leads through a hemlock forest, and past a series of rapids and pools, to end at an intersection with the High Peter's Kill Trail (blue) at its bridge crossing of the stream. The point is nearly a mile from the parking area. To return from here to the parking area, the hiker should take the trail back to the junction mentioned above. Here, one should turn uphill on a steep, eroded road that originally provided access to the ski slopes. Climbing several hundred feet above the valley floor, this road leads to open fields (once cleared for skiing), with exceptional views of the Catskills. After crossing the ridgetop, the trail continues along a dirt road that descends past low cliffs to the parking area.

Figure 6-18
Peter's Kill rapids.

7. MINNEWASKA-MILLBROOK

Millbrook Mountain and the Minnewaska highlands form the mid-section of the Shawangunks. The 4½-mile-long escarpment – from near the Trapps south to Gertrude's Nose – rises dramatically from the Wallkill Valley. Behind the cliffs are the upper valley of the Coxing Kill, Lake Minnewaska (rivaled only by Mohonk Lake for beauty) and the Awosting Falls of the Peter's Kill. Exploring this terrain is one of the great pleasures of the Shawangunks.

Route 44-55 is the northern boundary of this section. The escarpment forms the eastern and southeastern edge. Palmaghatt Ravine and Lake Minnewaska are to the south and west. The administration of this area is divided between the Minnewaska State Park Preserve and the Mohonk Preserve.

The basic geologic structure of this section of the Shawangunks consists of a northeast-plunging syncline that forms the valley of the Coxing Kill, and a less obvious anticline, the axis of which runs along Palmaghatt Ravine. These gentle folds in the topography are cut across by a number of faults – most in a northerly and northwesterly direction – that account for the trend of Lake Minnewaska, some of the notching in the southeastern cliff scarp, and the extreme angles of dip at Millbrook Mountain.

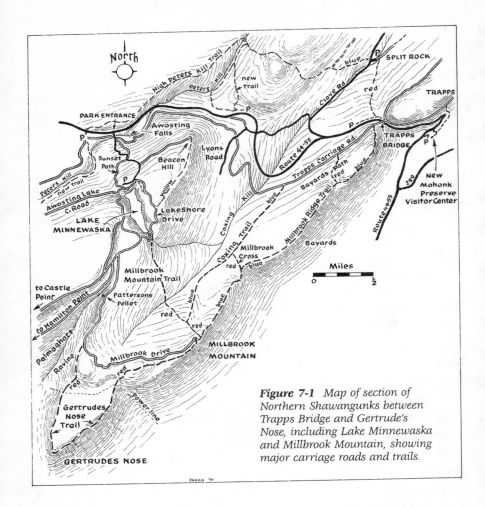

Figure 7-1 *Map of section of Northern Shawangunks between Trapps Bridge and Gertrude's Nose, including Lake Minnewaska and Millbrook Mountain, showing major carriage roads and trails.*

HISTORY

In 1879, Alfred H. Smiley opened the first of two mountain houses at Lake Minnewaska. This was nine years after his brother had opened the Mohonk Mountain House, five miles to the north. The first hotel at Minnewaska was built near the cliff edge east of the lake and came to be called the Cliff House. The second hotel was the Wildmere, built in 1887 at a lower elevation on the north end of the lake. Cliff House, long a landmark visible to travelers for miles around, burned in 1978. Wildmere was destroyed by fire in 1986.

The Minnewaska mountain houses were considered somewhat more rustic than the Mohonk resort. With its more than 10,000 acres, including Lake Awosting to the south, Minnewaska provided a wider and wilder terrain to be explored by its guests. In 1955, descendants of Alfred Smiley sold the property to Kenneth Phillips, the resort's general manager. Phillips proceeded to update the facility by adding a golf course in 1957 and "Ski-Minne," a downhill ski area, in 1963. However, the increasing costs of maintaining the old, wooden hotels and escalating taxes forced Phillips in 1971 to sell 7,000 acres, including Lake Awosting, to New York for a state park. At the time, he still hoped to construct a modern resort at Lake Minnewaska. But finances did not permit this, and eventually Phillips filed for bankruptcy. A number of lawsuits were filed by environmental groups opposing the impact of a new resort and, in 1987, the remaining property was acquired by the Palisades Interstate Park Commission.

Today, more than 10,000 acres comprise the Minnewaska State Park Preserve and are open to the public. Visitors can follow the old carriage roads that circle Lake Minnewaska and radiate out toward Lake Awosting, Millbrook Mountain and Mohonk. In addition to these century-old routes (designated as "carriageways" on Park signs and maps), today's hikers have a number of trails to choose from – footpaths that lead through pine barrens, along clifftops and into wooded glens *(see map: Figure 7-1)*. (These trails – along with some carriage roads that are no longer maintained – are designated on Park signs as "paths.") The carriage roads ("carriageways") in Minnewaska have been marked by the Park with colored diamond-shaped markers. These markers are primarily intended for skiers, and they generally will not be referred to in this book.

ACCESS

There are two principal locations for access to the Millbrook-Minnewaska area. Mohonk Preserve maintains a parking area on Route 44-55 just west of the Trapps Bridge. This parking area is a useful access point for hikers headed toward Millbrook Mountain or beyond to Gertrude's Nose. It is also used by hikers, bikers and skiers taking the Trapps Carriage Road to Awosting Falls and Lake Minnewaska. A per-person fee is charged to enter the Preserve lands.

Minnewaska State Park Preserve has three parking areas. One parking area is just west of the Park entrance on Route 44-55; another is near Lake Minnewaska, at the end of the paved access road leading to the lake. The third parking area is on Route 44-55, between Trapps Bridge and the

Figure 7-2 *Talus blocks at base of cliffs along east shore of Lake Minnewaska.*

Park entrance. This parking area, opened in 1996 to accommodate rock climbers and hikers using the trails along the Peter's Kill, was mentioned in the previous chapter. For most of the year, a per-car fee is charged (when cross-country skiing is available, there is a per-person fee). Most visitors to Minnewaska park near the lake and remain in that vicinity (*Figure 7-2*). The more adventurous use the lake area as a starting point to walk, bike or ski the old carriage roads toward Lake Awosting and Castle Point, or to Millbrook Mountain and Gertrude's Nose. The parking area on Route 44-55 near the Park entrance serves hikers walking to Awosting Falls or to more-distant Lake Awosting, as well as providing access to the High Peter's Kill Trail (see preceding chapter).

Figure 7-3
Awosting Falls on the Peter's Kill; near the main entrance to the Minnewaska State Park Preserve.

CARRIAGE ROADS

Trapps Carriage Road connects the Trapps area of the Mohonk Preserve with the entrance to Minnewaska State Park Preserve. (The portion of the road in the Park Preserve is also known as the **Awosting Falls Carriageway.**) From Trapps Bridge, the carriage road almost immediately passes the start of the Millbrook Ridge Trail (blue blazes). Beyond the trailhead, the carriage road crosses an exposure of gently-dipping conglomerate layers. A few millstones were once quarried here. About a mile from Trapps Bridge, another blue-blazed trail leads to the left (south). This is the Coxing Trail. The carriage road enters a dark hemlock glen and crosses the Coxing Kill over a wooden bridge. About 1¾ miles from Trapps Bridge, the carriage road crosses Lyons Road (watch for cars). Briefly, the carriage road becomes very rough until it passes a fork to a shale quarry. Resuming its normal surface quality, the road ascends a gentle slope and follows the base of a series of outcrops which rise in places to form cliffs. The old road is now very near Route 44-55, and traffic may be heard. Soon the highway is at hand on the right.

The carriage road angles away into a lovely hemlock forest and travels upstream alongside the Peter's Kill. In half a mile, the sound of falling water heralds Awosting Falls, one of the gems of the Shawangunks *(Figure 7-3)*. Here the Peter's Kill falls over a cliff of conglomerate into a deep pool that has enticed many a swimmer (but swimming is now forbidden). The carriage road curves upward near the base of the falls, climbing the cliff via a long, steep switchback to arrive at the spectacular edge of the falls. Several gazebos once stood at the edge of the precipice, allowing mountain house guests to enjoy dramatic views of the falling water. The carriage road continues upstream a short distance and ends at the paved lake access road. This point is about 3 miles from Trapps Bridge.

Sunset Carriage Road, an early access road to Lake Minnewaska, is now called **Sunset Path** on trail maps. It has been superseded by a paved automobile road which takes a slightly different route from the highway to the parking area near the lake. To follow Sunset Path as a continuation of the carriage road from Trapps Bridge, turn off the paved road almost immediately onto the old shale road ascending to the left. After a

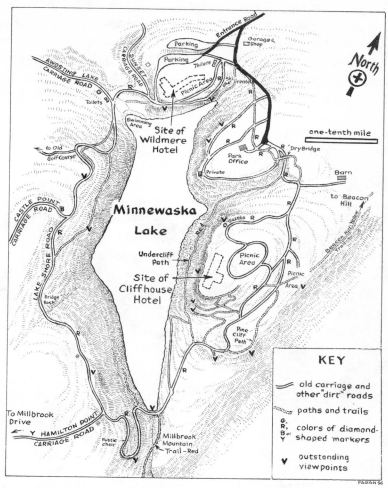

Figure 7-4 *Detail map of the Lake Minnewaska area.*

switchback, Sunset Path turns and crosses the paved road, heading west into the woods, snaking its way uphill. It crests the rise near an old frame house and descends briefly to meet Lake Shore Drive, another carriage road. This point is about a mile from the base of Awosting Falls and about 350 feet higher. The Sunset-Lake Shore intersection is just below the main lake parking area and about 25 feet above the lake level. There is a good view of Minnewaska's cerulean waters. The lake, at 1,650 feet above sea level, is naturally acidic and contains no fish. Snakes and amphibians, however, may occasionally be seen in or near the lake.

Lake Shore Drive (also known as **Minnewaska Carriageway**) was constructed as a carriage road to allow guests of the Minnewaska mountain houses, as well as visitors from Mohonk, to circle the half-mile-long

Figure 7-5 "Ghost" of Cliff House. Outline of the former resort hotel atop the present cliffline, east side of Lake Minnewaska.

lake. Because of its curves and switchbacks, the road takes almost two miles to complete the circuit *(see map: Figure 7-4)*. Today, a small segment is used for automobile access to the Park office, but almost all of it remains a fine route for walking and biking or for skiing in snow season.

To follow Lake Shore Drive counterclockwise around the lake, turn right (west) from the Sunset intersection, descending a short distance to an intersection with the Awosting Lake Carriage Road (several chemical toilets may be found at this intersection). Lake Awosting, the largest of the Sky Lakes, is 3½ miles away via this road. Nearby is the swimming area, heavily used in summer. Lake Shore Drive continues by climbing steeply via a switchback and then more gently to reach an intersection with the Castle Point Carriage Road. Castle Point is three miles away along this route.

Soon there is a view of the lake. In the heyday of the resort, this was an especially popular drive. The trees were kept well-trimmed to provide continuous views across the lake to Cliff House, perched 130 feet above the lake. Today, the trees have regrown and Cliff House is gone, but the views that do occur are all the better for their pristine quality, as if returned to a time centuries ago (*Figure 7-5*).

Additional lake views are encountered along the Drive before meeting the start of the Hamilton Point Carriage Road. Hamilton Point is about the same distance from the lake as Castle Point. Both have striking cliff edges with panoramic views and are described in the next section.

From this intersection at the southeastern end of the lake, Lake Shore Drive descends several switchback curves, passing a rustic chair to arrive at the lake edge. The carriage road, almost at water level, crosses a dam of glacial boulders that impound the lake at this end. The waters that do drain through these boulders are the headwaters of a branch of the Coxing Kill. The red-blazed Millbrook Mountain Trail starts here and follows the little stream downhill.

Lake Shore Drive continues past a short branch road that leads along the shore to an old water pumping station. At a right-angled bend a little further along the Drive, a trail leads to the left (north). This is Undercliff Path. Now mostly unmarked, this old trail follows the base of the cliff and crosses a rock scramble below the site of Cliff House. Lake Shore Drive ascends steeply, passing unmarked Pine Cliff Path on the right, with good views to the east, and arrives at a picnic area. This was the lawn of Cliff House. The hotel was located just to the west. Paths lead to the cliff edge and to a single gazebo (*Figure 7-6*). There used to be dozens of these structures scattered around the resort for use by guests. This is the only one left.

The terrain to the east and north of Lake Minnewaska has many old paths leading to former hotel entrances or outbuildings and to barns and viewpoints. Some of these make for interesting exploration. To the east of the Drive, across another grassy lawn, is the beginning of the yellow-blazed Beacon Hill Trail.

North of the Cliff House area, Lake Shore Drive passes under Dry Bridge *(Figure 7-7)*, an overpass for walkers, and turns into a paved road. The road may be avoided by using the adjacent path. To return to the

Figure 7-6
Last of Minnewaska's summerhouses, or gazebos, overlooking the lake.

Sunset intersection, turn left onto the shale road paralleling the lake edge, but avoid the path down to the water's edge. Looking back towards the southeast, one cannot fail to see a modern stone house perched on the cliff edge near the current Park office. This building was constructed by the Phillipses in 1987 – about the time the state took possession of Lake Minnewaska – for their private residence. The main parking area for lake visitors is next to a picnic area, just above Lake Shore Drive, which was the site of Wildmere.

Beacon Hill Carriage Road leads to a viewpoint on the ledges of Beacon Hill, a northeastern spur of the Lake Minnewaska heights. It branches off the automobile access road about 1,000 feet from the parking area at the lake. The carriage road is about half a mile long. The viewpoint is also the terminus of the yellow-blazed Beacon Hill Trail. From here, the Trapps ridge line may be seen beyond the valley of the Coxing Kill.

Millbrook Drive (also known as the **Millbrook Mountain Carriageway**) is a carriage road that begins at the Hamilton Point Carriage Road near the lake and ends at the cliff edge of Millbrook Mountain. Millbrook's cliffs measure some 500 feet from base to top, the greatest vertical drop in the Shawangunks. The cliff face is highly visible from many miles to the east. From its beginning near the head of Palmaghatt Ravine, about half a mile from Lake Shore Drive, Millbrook Drive winds along the edge of low cliffs bordering the ravine. Not far along is a large boulder – a glacial erratic – known as

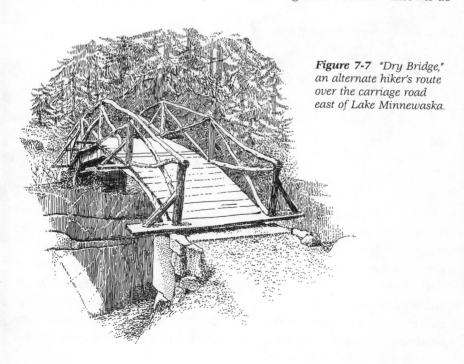

Figure 7-7 "Dry Bridge," an alternate hiker's route over the carriage road east of Lake Minnewaska.

Patterson's Pellet, which is picturesquely perched on the smooth white clifftop surface *(Figure 7-8)*. Palmaghatt Ravine below is the head of a long valley that cuts through the Shawangunk Conglomerate and deep into the Ordovician shales. In earlier times, several trails followed precarious routes into its depth. Rarely explored today, the Ravine is a region of massive talus boulders, waterfalls, and dense hemlock forest.

Figure 7-8
Patterson's Pellet, a glacial erratic boulder on cliff edge overlooking Palmaghatt Ravine.

Beyond the Pellet, the carriage road passes more glacial boulders *(Figure 7-9)* and the beginning of a red-blazed trail. The latter is the Gertrude's Nose Trail, which continues to follow the edge of the ravine, while the carriage road turns into the woods. Elevations here reach over 1,800 feet. Continuing eastward, the road gradually descends and nears the edge of the easternmost cliff scarp of the Shawangunks. For the last quarter of a mile, the cliffs are near at hand, and the red blazes of the northern end of Gertrude's Nose Trail may be seen between the road and the cliff edge.

The carriage road ends at a turnaround. Several stone steps carved into the bedrock surface lead to an overlook from the clifftop. This is the summit of Millbrook Mountain, about 1,600 feet above sea level. Views of the Wallkill Valley and the Hudson Valley beyond are excellent. It is not surprising to find iron anchors, the remains of long-vanished gazebos, at several spots along the top of Millbrook Mountain. Several hiking trails converge in this vicinity. It is the terminus of the blue-blazed Millbrook Ridge Trail. The blue markings may be seen just north of the road's end. By following these a very short distance, the beginning of the red-blazed Millbrook Mountain Trail may be found. The red-blazed Gertrude's Nose Trail also ends at the turnaround of the carriage road.

Figure 7-9 *Erratic boulders left by Ice Age glaciers: Millbrook Drive*

Figure 7-10
*Great boulder field at the
base of Millbrook Mountain*

TRAILS

Millbrook Ridge Trail connects the Trapps Bridge area with Millbrook Mountain, a distance of about 2 ¾ miles. For much of its length, it is a cliff-edge trail. Millbrook Mountain is about 600 feet higher than Trapps Bridge. There are a number of ups and downs along the way, so that the total climb is considerably greater than 600 feet. Most of the trail passes over conglomerate ledges and through the sparse growth of pitch pine and small oaks so typical of the clifftops of the Shawangunks.

The northern end of this footpath is on the Trapps Carriage Road, a few hundred feet south of Trapps Bridge. From here, the blue-blazed trail climbs steeply over bare, sloping conglomerate surfaces, gaining about 200 feet of elevation to reach an open ridge, known as the Near Trapps. This crest offers fine views of Dickie Barre, the Trapps cliffs and Undercliff Road. To the north is a panorama of the Catskills, and to the east are New Paltz and the Wallkill Valley. This is a favorite spot for watching the fall migration of hawks and other soaring birds. A short distance ahead are outcrops showing good examples of glacial striations and chattermarks produced by the passage of the glaciers. The trail continues along this ridgetop, then descends into a notch, with a red-blazed trail coming in from the right. This is Bayard's Path, a half-mile-long connecting trail that allows a return to the Trapps Carriage Road.

The blue blazes continue ahead as the trail climbs 100 feet onto Bayard's Ridge. Among the gnarled pine are more examples of glacial erosion. Striations are widespread, and many of the pebbles in exposed conglomerate layers have been ground down to a smooth, common level. The trail descends again into a more heavily wooded terrain and meets another red-blazed trail – the Millbrook Cross Path. This short route leads to the Coxing Trail, about a third of a mile to the west. The Millbrook Ridge Trail leaves this notch and climbs a narrow ridge made of layers of conglomerate turned up at steep angles, some nearly vertical. These high dip angles, very unusual in the Shawangunk conglomerate, indicate the proximity of a fault zone cutting across the ridge in this area.

The trail climbs higher on the narrow ridgetop, passing more excellent viewpoints. Using great caution, it is possible to peer over the sharp cliff edges and glimpse the vast boulder field found below the Millbrook cliffs *(Figure 7-10)*. These piles of rocks are so much greater in scale than talus accumulations at the base of other cliffs – even considering that the Millbrook cliffs are twice as high as most cliffs in the Shawangunks – that an explanation other than the usual gravity collapse is called for. Most likely, these boulder fields mark the location of the outer margin of a separate mass of glacial ice that persisted under the cliff scarp long after the main ice sheet melted away. They are, in effect, a moraine formed of rocks plucked from the cliff by the action of this remnant glacier and indicate its outer edge as it melted away in slow stages.

The Millbrook Ridge Trail ends near the turnaround of Millbrook Drive. Here, too, is one end of the red-blazed Gertrude's Nose Trail. About 200 feet before the end of the Millbrook Ridge Trail is an intersection with the red-blazed Millbrook Mountain Trail, another means of access to this location. Hikers in this area should consult the map to avoid confusing one red-blazed trail with another.

Coxing Trail, marked with blue blazes, is roughly parallel to the Millbrook Ridge Trail. For most of its 1½-mile length, it runs through thick forest, following an old road through the valley of the Coxing Kill. The

Figure 7-11
Rock-enclosed spring
near Coxing Trail

Figure 7-12
*Carriage road at south end of
Lake Minnewaska: start of
Millbrook Mountain Trail.*

northern end is on the Trapps Carriage Road, one mile from Trapps Bridge; its southern terminus is on the red-blazed Millbrook Mountain Trail, near the Millbrook overlook. The south end of Coxing Trail is in an open area of exposed rock and dwarf pines. Excellent views toward Sky Top and the Trapps reward hikers leaving Millbrook Mountain by this route as the trail descends northward over ledges of conglomerate. The dense mountain laurel in this valley makes it an enchanting hike in June.

Rock outcrops gradually fade into thicker soils, and the forest closes in. This land was once farmed, and old stone walls are still visible near the trail. An observant hiker will be able to find a rock-enclosed spring just to the left (west) of the trail *(Figure 7-11)*, perhaps developed to water livestock. Once cleared and sunny, this area has now reverted to hardwood forest. Only the stone walls and piles of rocks removed from old fields remain as reminders of its history. The Coxing Trail ends at the Trapps Carriage Road. A right turn leads to Trapps Bridge; a left crosses the Coxing Kill and leads toward Minnewaska.

Millbrook Mountain Trail is marked with red blazes and should not be confused with the Millbrook Ridge Trail, which is blazed blue. The Millbrook Mountain Trail is about one mile long; it connects Lake Minnewaska with Millbrook Mountain. Although it is the shortest route between these two popular locations, it is not the easiest one. The trail has a half-mile descent and a corresponding ascent, each involving roughly 300 feet of elevation.

The northwestern end of the trail is at Lake Shore Drive where the old carriage road rounds the southern end of the lake *(Figure 7-12)*. At the outlet of the lake, red blazes lead down over a mass of boulders. At the foot of a long slope, the path reaches a pleasant, mossy glen, through which flows a branch of the Coxing Kill *(Figure 7-13)*. Across the stream, the trail ascends the eastern side of the valley. This section of the trail is usually damp and slippery. The soil is extremely thin and in places has been eroded away to expose the glacially-scoured surface of the conglomerate beneath. In this synclinal valley, the rock layers dip (angle downward) toward the valley bottom. The combination of tilted rock and glacial smoothing makes for a hazardous trail, especially in icy and wet conditions.

Finally, the trail emerges into an open area of scattered pines and lowbush blueberries. At the junction with Coxing Trail (blue blazes), there are excellent views to the north. Along the red trail, the slope

Figure 7-13 *Coxing Kill*
at the crossing of
Millbrook Mountain Trail.

steepens considerably, reflecting an increasing angle of dip of the rock layers underfoot. One quarter of a mile beyond the Coxing Trail intersection, the Millbrook Mountain Trail ends at another junction, this time with the Millbrook Ridge Trail (blue blazes). The cliff edge of Millbrook Mountain, with its magnificent views, is just ahead *(Figure 7-14)*. The turnaround of the old carriage road is to the right.

Figure 7-14 *View south from Millbrook Mountain: Sky Top in distance.*

Gertrude's Nose Trail, red-blazed and a little over two miles long, leads to Gertrude's Nose. An odd name for a unique place, the Nose is a great wedge-like mass of conglomerate left between Palmaghatt Ravine and the main cliff scarp south of Millbrook Mountain *(Figure 7-15)*. The trail makes a triangle, with Millbrook Drive as its base and Gertrude's Nose as the apex. This little-used trail is one of the finest clifftop routes in the Shawangunks *(Figure 7-16)*.

The western end of the trail starts at Millbrook Drive about 1¹⁄₂ miles from Lake Minnewaska. It heads south near the cliff edge through a dense growth of hemlocks and down a steep slope to cross a small stream that drains into Palmaghatt Ravine. Power lines are overhead here. The trail then climbs along the edge of the cliffs that bound the Ravine. Intricate joint cracks widen into deep intersection crevices. Huge blocks of conglomerate lie at random angles below the cliffs *(Figure 7-17)*. Ahead, the Nose itself is shaped like the prow of a great stone ship. Because of the 45° angle formed by the cliff scarps, the views to the east and south are especially fine.

From Gertrude's Nose *(Figure 7-18)*, the trail continues parallel to the main line of cliffs. It is set back from the edge, more in the woods, with

Figure 7-15
View east from near Hamilton Point. Gertrude's Nose is seen as the terminus of the distant line of cliffs (arrow).

Figure 7-16
Hikers on the
Gertrude's Nose
Trail looking over
Palmaghatt Ravine.

only occasional views. Crossing the power lines again, the trail goes into a notch and then ascends to a level, scoured rock surface scattered with pines. Soon, Millbrook Drive angles in from the left. The red blazes end near the turnaround terminus of the carriage road at the summit of Millbrook Mountain. Here also are the blue blazes that mark the southern end of the Millbrook Ridge Trail.

Figure 7-17
*Tilted blocks of conglomerate
bedrock along the Gertrude's Nose Trail.*

Beacon Hill Trail, yellow-blazed and about ¾ mile long, begins in the grassy meadow east of Lake Shore Drive near the site of the old Cliff House. Along this pleasant trail are a number of ledges with good views to the east. It ends at the viewpoint on Beacon Hill, which is also the terminus of the old carriage road. Combining the Beacon Hill Carriage Road and Beacon Hill Trail with Lake Shore Drive – plus a short stretch of the paved access road – makes an easy circular hike of about 1¾ miles from the parking area near the lake.

There are also other trails near Lake Minnewaska. During the days of Minnewaska's mountain houses, a great number of footpaths came into existence. Undercliff and Pine Cliff Paths and other routes were established to explore the area around Cliff House. Several short spurs were established on the opposite side of the lake, leading to ledges with

Figure 7-18 *Outlook at Gertrude's Nose.*

good views across the water. Most of these trails were not marked, and they are not maintained today, but may be followed by the patient and curious walker.

8. AWOSTING

AWOSTING

A mile and a quarter in length, Lake Awosting is the largest of the five mountaintop Sky Lakes. Its elevation is 1,867 feet above sea level; only Lake Maratanza is higher. Adjacent to Lake Awosting (or within a mile of it) are to be found perhaps the greatest number of ledges, cliffs and viewpoints in the Shawangunks. These include Castle Point, Hamilton Point, Battlement Terrace, Margaret Cliff and Murray Hill – all outlooks with fine views.

Throughout this area, the conglomerate beds dip northwestward, and two distinct upper and lower cliff-forming units may be recognized. The lower beds that comprise Hamilton Point dip downward under the upper beds that form Castle Point. The lower unit, stretching southwest from Hamilton Point, has been eroded into two wedge-shaped promontories called Murray Hill and Margaret Cliff *(Figure 8-1)*. Between the two is Spruce Glen, cut into underlying shales. Two waterfalls, Rainbow and Stony Kill, the deep valley called Huntington Ravine, and the cascading upper Peter's Kill are other scenic features that reward the hiker venturing into this relatively remote area.

Lake Awosting is appealing throughout the year. In the fall, the lake is set in an array of autumn reds and yellows interspersed with evergreens. Migrating waterfowl sometimes rest on the lake during their journeys. In summer, Awosting's cool waters invite the weary walker onto the sloping rock "beach" on the southeast shore. In winter, the frozen lake becomes a great white meadow framed in dark hemlocks and pines *(Figure 8-2)*.

HISTORY

Lake Awosting was originally known as Long Pond. Once acquired by Alfred Smiley and renamed, it became an appealing destination for guests of the Minnewaska Mountain Houses, some three miles to the north. The Awosting Lake Carriage Road was built to allow carriages to reach and circle the lake. In 1903, a camp for boys, known as Camp Awosting, was established on the west side of the lake. For many years, the camp prospered; in the 1950s, it was succeeded by Camp Laurel.

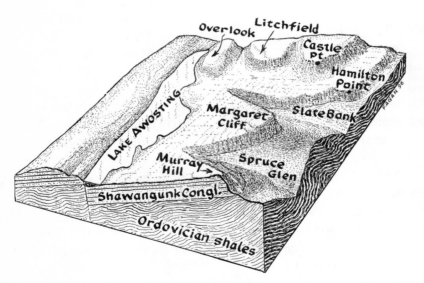

Figure 8-1 *Block diagram showing how the gently-dipping, lower Shawangunk conglomerate layers have been eroded into the landforms known as Murray Hill, Margaret Cliff and Hamilton Point. Castle Point and Litchfield Ledge are remnant areas of higher, overlying layers of the Shawangunk Conglomerate.*

Figure 8-2 *Lake Awosting, from the east.*

The Castle Point and Hamilton Point Carriage Roads were constructed along the cliff edges as scenic drives between Lake Minnewaska and the
Lake Awosting area. They became extremely popular routes for day excursions by guests at Wildmere and the Cliff House. By way of these drives,
the guests enjoyed the variety of spectacular views looking east over the
Wallkill Valley on their way to the circular drive around Lake Awosting.

Near the foot of the road to Lake Minnewaska was a smaller hotel,
the Laurel Inn. This was a modest guest house built in the 1870s to
accommodate visitors unable to afford the grander hotels above. The inn
was destroyed in the 1960s, and the site is now the Awosting parking area.

ACCESS

Unlike the areas around Lakes Mohonk and Minnewaska, the
Awosting area is relatively remote. The lake itself is over three miles by
foot or bicycle from the nearest access. There are two parking areas along
Route 44-55 – one, known as the Awosting parking area, just west of the
entrance to Minnewaska State Park Preserve, and another at Jenny Lane,
a little farther west. The parking area adjacent to Lake Minnewaska itself
– less than a mile drive from the highway – provides a starting point at a
higher elevation. For the very sturdy hiker, access from Ellenville, seven
miles to the southwest, is a possibility.

CARRIAGE ROADS

The **Jenny Lane Trail,** now part of the Long Path, has been the only footpath connecting the lake area with a distant parking area. A proposed (1997) footpath will connect the Awosting parking area with the Blueberry Run Trail, thus providing another trail route to Lake Awosting. Nevertheless, old carriage roads remain an important means of access. The parking area on Route 44-55 just west of Minnewaska entrance was the starting point used by most visitors between 1971 – when New York State acquired the Awosting section – and 1987, when Lake Minnewaska was added to the Park Preserve. It is about three miles along the Peter's Kill Carriage Road (also known as Lower Awosting Carriageway) from the parking area to the lake, and it is approximately the same distance from the Lake Minnewaska parking area to Lake Awosting via the Awosting Lake Carriage Road (also known as the Upper Awosting Carriageway) *(see map: Figure 8-3).*

AROUND THE LAKE

Once at Awosting, it is possible to circumnavigate the lake on the **Awosting Lake Shore Road,** also known as the Awosting Carriageway *(see map: Figure 8-4).* This should not be undertaken lightly, however, because the route is some three miles long. Although nearly level for much of the way, the road makes many switchbacks as it negotiates Overlook Hill at the northeastern end of the lake.

Starting clockwise from the swimming area, the road at first closely follows the shoreline. Visible ahead and across the lake are outcrops and a beaver lodge hugging the lake edge. The carriage road makes a sharp bend well beyond the south end of the lake. Just before this turn, a short stretch of the Long Path joins the road, coming in from Murray Hill, and almost immediately leaves again, heading uphill toward Mud Pond, a mile away to the south. From the bend, the carriage road heads northeast, rising over conglomerate outcrops. On the left are faint remains of the old Camp Awosting. Continuing along the shore, the road passes the widest part of the lake and reaches the Old Smiley Carriage Road which comes in from the west (left). This road provided access from the Village of Ellenville to Lake Awosting.

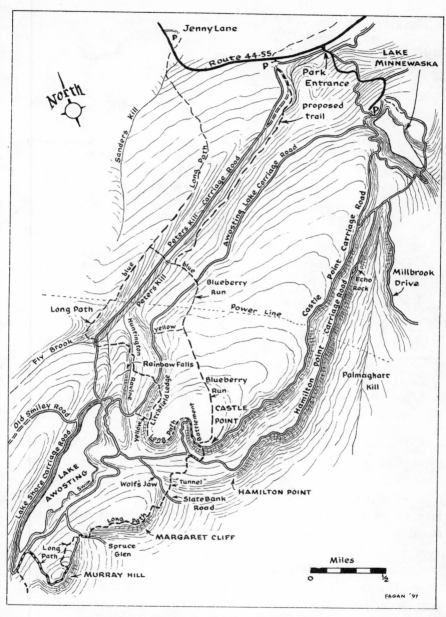

Figure 8-3 Map of Lake Awosting section.

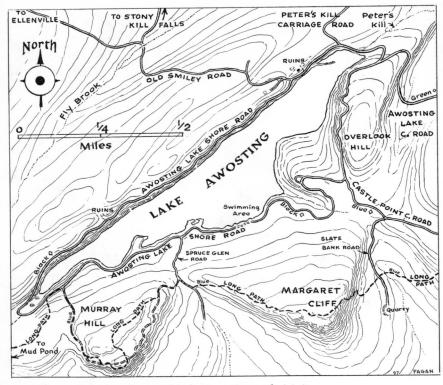

Figure 8-4 *Detail map of Lake Awosting and vicinity.*

The lower part of the Old Smiley Road was much used by blueberry pickers prior to the 1950s. Ellenville is about seven miles from Lake Awosting via this now badly eroded and little used road. Stony Kill Falls *(Figure 8-5)* may be visited by taking this route. Less than a mile from the lake, where the Old Smiley Road crosses Fly Brook, **Stony Kill Carriage Road** branches off to the right. In just over a mile more, the Stony Kill Road ends near the top of the falls. Stony Kill Falls, which drains the slab-lands or pine plains, drops 87 feet over conglomerate ledges. It can also be reached from below by walking in along Shaft Road, which branches from Rock Haven Road 2½ miles from Route 44-55. There is no marked trail from the base to the top of the falls.

Figure 8-5
Stony Kill Falls.

Continuing around the lake, the Awosting Lake Shore Road passes below the sometime-ranger station, once the infirmary of Camp Laurel, and comes to an old clearing with camp remains. Here the **Peter's Kill Carriage Road** (also known as the Lower Awosting Carriageway) comes in from the left. The Peter's Kill Road, a relatively uninteresting route, well-worn by past vehicular traffic and open to the sun, leads three miles to the parking area on Route 44-55. Next, the outlet of the lake is crossed; this is the head of the Peter's Kill stream. Soon, the well-engineered **Awosting Lake Carriage Road** (also known as the Upper Awosting Carriageway) comes in from the left at an acute angle. (It leads three miles to Lake Minnewaska.) To complete the circumnavigation of Awosting, continue southeastward on the lakeshore route, marked with black diamonds. The road gradually climbs Overlook Hill and passes some ruins, including the collapsed remains of a barn. The carriage road twists its way along, rising higher by a series of switchbacks that afford constantly improving views of Lake Awosting and the cliffs above the shore. The clifftops here provide evidence of the Ice Age, showing the polishing, striations and other marks of the glaciers more than 12,000 years ago. Near the crest of the hill, the curious walker will be able to find a cleverly laid-out bridle path that curves off toward higher ground and leads to excellent vistas on the east side of the hilltop. This once-shaled and built-up path has narrowed to about a foot wide, but it is well worth exploring.

The clockwise route around the lake soon encounters another major intersection. To the left is the carriage road leading to Castle Point and Hamilton Point. Continuing to the right, the shore road (black diamond markers) descends in sweeping curves to the lake again. The last stretch of road follows the water's edge to reach the swimming area. Primitive comfort stations are located here, and a lifeguard is on duty during the summer months.

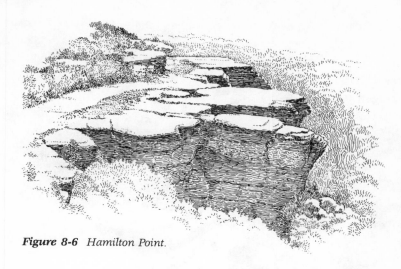

Figure 8-6 *Hamilton Point.*

CASTLE POINT AND HAMILTON POINT

The much-used **Castle Point Carriage Road** connects the Lake Awosting area with two spectacular viewpoints: Castle Point and (indirectly) Hamilton Point *(Figure 8-6)*. Starting at a sharp bend in the Awosting Lake Shore Road between the swimming area and Overlook Hill, this carriage road heads southeastward. Marked by blue triangles, it rises gradually in a series of curves through pine-birch woods. Soon an intersection is reached where an unmarked road goes to the right. This is the half-mile-long Slate Bank Road, once used to reach a shale (not slate) quarry that supplied material for road maintenance.

An interesting side trip may be made down the Slate Bank Road toward the quarry. The road passes under the Wolf Jaw, a cliff face where slabs of conglomerate hang dramatically over the road *(Figure 8-7)*. This location offers an opportunity to compare the two basic geologic formations of the region: the conglomerates seen in the cliffs, and the older shales in the nearby quarry. Between the Wolf Jaw and the shale quarry, Slate Bank Road intersects the Long Path, giving the walker an alternate route northward to the Castle Point Road or the opportunity to make a much longer circular walk over Margaret Cliff and back to Lake Awosting.

Figure 8-7 *The Wolf Jaw.*
This ledge overhangs Slate
Bank Road near the crossing
of the Long Path.

From the intersection of Slate Bank Road, Castle Point Carriage Road continues east on a curving ascent. In winter, the cliffs of Battlement Terrace are visible through the trees ahead *(Figure 8-8)*. Shortly after a bare rock clearing on the right, there is a major carriage road intersection. Just before this junction, turquoise blazes appear, as the Long Path, coming from ahead, turns sharply right off the road and heads south. The choice here is whether to take the carriage road to Hamilton Point ahead or the one to Castle Point, a sharp left.

Figure 8-8 Battlement Terrace, seen from the west.

The **Hamilton Point Carriage Road** is marked with yellow diamonds with a small, superimposed "H." It is about half a mile from the carriage road junction to Hamilton Point. The Long Path follows this road for a short distance before turning left to make a rock scramble climb to Castle Point above. The last part of the carriage road follows the cliff edge. At Hamilton Point, there is an awesome variety of natural stone architecture caused by the slumping of great blocks of conglomerate and the widening of deep joint crevices. Beyond Hamilton Point, the carriage road continues past many fine viewpoints en route to Lake Minnewaska *(Figure 8-9)*. One of these is Echo Rock, a spectacular slab overhanging Palmaghatt Ravine.

The Castle Point Carriage Road takes the walker through a narrowing "canyon" that ascends Battlement Terrace. This segment of old road is built on large blocks of roughly hewn conglomerate *(Figure 8-10)*. Just before a sharp bend, the turquoise paint blazes of the Long Path appear on the left as that trail joins the road. Finally, the road reaches a level

Figure 8-9
Pinnacled cliff edge formed by intersecting joint crevices along the Hamilton Point Carriage Road.

Figure 8-10
The cliffs of Battlement Terrace overhang the old carriage road that curves upward to reach Castle Point.

Figure 8-11
Rock pinnacle near the Castle Point Carriage Road. Erosion along joint cracks has allowed the collapse of rock masses on either side of this remnant of the slowly-receding cliff face.

grade – the top of Battlement Terrace. The huge rectangular blocks and deep joint crevices make the name seem appropriate. The road winds along the irregular clifftop, with fine views, and finally arrives at Castle Point, the highest elevation. This summit is much visited by hikers and bikers, skiers in winter and family outings in summer. It is one of the outstanding places on the Long Path, and it is also the southern terminus of the recently-established Blueberry Run Trail.

If Castle Point is too crowded with nature seekers, there are many other clifftop overlooks ahead along the carriage road as it continues towards Lake Minnewaska *(Figure 8-11)*. About 1½ miles from Castle Point, a fork in the road is reached. The branch down to the right soon intersects the Hamilton Point Road, descends to Millbrook Drive, and continues beyond toward the south end of Lake Minnewaska. Ahead, the carriage road gradually descends for ⅓ mile to Lake Shore Drive, a short distance from the parking area at the north end of the lake.

TRAILS

The principal marked footpath in this section of the Shawangunks is the turquoise-blazed **Long Path,** which incorporates the old Scenic Trail. The spectacular, five-mile-long Scenic Trail was laid out decades ago by Maurice Avery, a member of the New York-New Jersey Trail Conference. It was originally marked with yellow blazes, some of which can still be seen. Stretching from Fly Brook on the north to the south end of Lake Awosting, the Scenic Trail zigzags over the rolling Shawangunk terrain. Along the way, the hiker traverses the great, jutting rock masses called Margaret Cliff and Murray Hill, climbs the ramparts of Castle Point and walks the spectacular ledges of Battlement Terrace. Some details of this delightful trail follow, starting at the south end.

The Long Path approaches Lake Awosting from Mud Pond (see following section) by dropping down over low ledges scattered with pitch pines. It reaches the Awosting Lake Shore Road near the south end of the lake. After following the carriage road to the right for several hundred feet, the trail turns sharply right and ascends another carriage road, Murray Hill Drive, which gradually climbs a series of northwest-dipping conglomerate layers to arrive at the cliff edges of Murray Hill. The old shale road is faded by erosion here, and the Long Path no longer follows it exactly.

Nearing the top of Murray Hill, walkers find on their left a separate higher outcrop. Topped by a boulder of glacial origin, this height provides excellent views. Continuing along the ledges, the Long Path reaches still another major outlook, with unobstructed views in all directions. Lake Awosting lies to the north, with Sam's Point to the southwest. Many of the high peaks of the Catskills are visible, and far to the south the outline of the Hudson Highlands may be seen.

The Long Path continues northward, in places coinciding with the worn carriage road. This pleasant route descends over a ledgy, dipping surface, eventually turning right onto the better-preserved Spruce Glen Drive. Spruce Glen, bisected by a short, dead-end road, is a marshy woods with red spruce, ancient hemlocks, a talus block cave called Margaret's Stone Parlor, and a small shale quarry. However, after a short distance on Spruce Glen Drive, the Long Path turns left and uphill over ledges to reach a narrow, shale-covered track that undulates upwards to Margaret Cliff, a land form similar in outline and origin to Murray Hill *(see Figure 8-1)*.

Margaret Cliff has a long eroded edge, with several sharp drop-offs and good views. The shale path soon fades away, but the turquoise markers lead the walker along the cliff to a point where the Long Path descends steeply amid ledges and crevices to the base of the pile of strata that comprises the wall of the Cliff.

Winding through talus blocks and glacial boulders, the trail reaches Slate Bank Road, which it crosses. (Uphill a short distance is the Wolf Jaw, described above.) After crossing a small stream – the headwaters of the Dwaar Kill – the trail begins a climb through thick forest. It reaches an area of outcrops and strewn talus blocks where the turquoise markers lead the walker through a tunnel-like maze of huge conglomerate boulders to emerge into a shelter cave *(Figure 8-12)*. A less agile walker can avoid the tunnel by an obvious detour. Upslope, the trail reaches a carriage road and turns right.

Immediately ahead is an important intersection. The Hamilton Point Carriage Road goes to the right, while the Castle Point Carriage Road branches left. By taking the left fork, one can bypass a steep, rocky climb and reach the top of Castle Point by a longer, easier route. The

Figure 8-12
The Tunnel,
a crevice along
the Long Path
between the
Castle Point
Carriage Road
and Slate
Bank Road.

Long Path, however, follows the Hamilton Point Road for about 600 feet before turning abruptly left off the road. The trail begins to rise over a steep, bouldery slope and climbs outcrops of the cliff base *(Figure 8-13)*. Next, a dramatic series of natural steps and handholds brings the intrepid hiker to the summit of Castle Point (elevation 2,200 feet), with its

Figure 8-13 *Climbing to Castle Point on the Long Path.*
The distant cliffs are Hamilton Point.

excellent view of the Wallkill Valley and beyond to the Hudson Highlands. Nearby, across the carriage road, is the southern terminus of the Blueberry Run Trail, which is marked with blue blazes (darker than the turquoise blazes of the Long Path).

At Castle Point, the Long Path turns left (north) on the carriage road. The old shale road twists along the cliff edge, soon arriving at an overlook, with striking exposures of the conglomerate layers cut into blocks by joint planes and crevices. This is Battlement Terrace, a good place to observe the effects of glaciers on the quartzite rock, including striations and polishing. The road curves downward. After a sharp bend, the turquoise blazes lead off into the woods to the right and

Figure 8-14
Litchfield Ledge, along the Long Path,
has fine views toward the Catskills.

across bare expanses of white strata en route to Litchfield Ledge.

About one mile from Castle Point, the Long Path reaches a trail junction. Ahead are yellow blazes; blue blazes lead to the right. The Long Path was rerouted here in 1994 in order to avoid a walk on the Awosting Lake Carriage Road, which is heavily used by bicyclists and skiers. The yellow blazes lead directly to the carriage road, passing a splendid view of many Catskill peaks from Litchfield Ledge *(Figure 8-14)*. The new route of the Long Path turns away from the Ledge, descends a little, and continues more or less on the level through a dense stand of tree-like mountain laurel. After passing a fine viewpoint to the north and west, the new trail descends to reach the Awosting Lake Carriage Road. (To the right, it is 2½ miles to the parking area at Lake Minnewaska). The Long Path

Figure 8-15 *Rainbow Falls, seen from its base, near the Long Path in Huntington Ravine.*

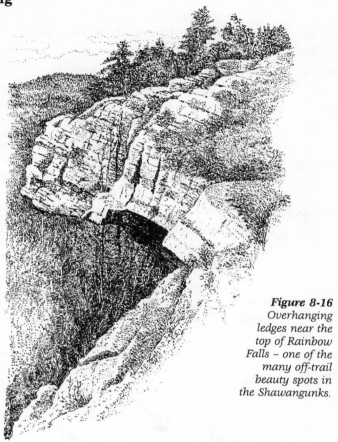

Figure 8-16
Overhanging
ledges near the
top of Rainbow
Falls – one of the
many off-trail
beauty spots in
the Shawangunks.

cuts directly across the road and curves down into the deep, heavily-wooded valley called Huntington Ravine. Steep cliffs rise near the trail as it passes through stands of birch, beech and hemlock.

The Long Path heads down the ravine toward the brook. After crossing it on mossy boulders or a fallen tree trunk, the hiker arrives at a waterfall cascading down a cliff face onto fallen rock fragments. This is Rainbow Falls, named for the colors occasionally seen in the mist produced by the chaotic dispersion of its waters as they are splashed into the air *(Figure 8-15)*.

From Rainbow Falls, the Long Path turns downstream and parallels the cliffs that frame the ravine on the northwest *(Figure 8-16)*. After several hundred yards, the trail ascends amid ledges and pinnacles of rock, passing several old red metal disks on trees. Reaching more level ground, it opens onto a superb view of the Catskills. From here, the turquoise blazes lead the walker down a gentle pavement – the top of a thick, dipping layer of conglomerate – to the Peter's Kill, with its shaded pools and rapids. Crossing this stream and following cairns, the Long Path soon comes out on the Peter's Kill Carriage Road and turns right. (From this point, it is 2½ miles to the Awosting parking area on Route 44-55.)

This was the end of the old Scenic Trail. The Long Path now heads north on the Peter's Kill Carriage Road, crossing a long earthen dam across Fly Brook, which is the outlet of distant Mud Pond. Just after the stream crossing, the trail turns into a clearing on the left side of the road. From here to Route 44-55, the Long Path follows the route of the old Jenny Lane Trail. It ascends a gentle slope, and descends again to cross a power line clearing. Reentering the woods, the Long Path follows an asymmetrical ridge with a steep, ledgy southeastern slope. In about one mile from the Peter's Kill Carriage Road, the Blueberry Run Trail comes in from the right. This is the northern end of this trail. Ahead, the Long Path descends toward the Jenny Lane parking area, just off Route 44-55, about two miles away.

Figure 8-17 *Rock cairn along the Blueberry Run Trail north of Castle Point.*

The **Blueberry Run Trail** connects Castle Point with the ridgetop west of the Peter's Kill. It can be reached via the Peter's Kill Carriage Road, which it intersects 1½ miles from Route 44-55. About three miles long, the trail is marked with blue paint, somewhat darker than the turquoise blazes of the Long Path. The Blueberry Run Trail may be used as part of a circular walk because, at each end, it intersects the Long Path. Blueberry Run also makes a handy connection between the parallel Peter's Kill and Awosting Lake Carriage Roads, and it provides an alternate route to Castle Point.

At Castle Point, the start of the Blueberry Run Trail may be difficult to find. It is located just off the Castle Point Carriage Road, about 80 feet north of where the Long Path drops over the edge of the cliff. Starting from the carriage road at three blue blazes, the trail heads into a forest of pitch pine, with outcrops of the white, glacially-scoured conglomerate. Turning northward, the trail is well-marked by neat blue rectangles and frequent cairns *(Figure 8-17).* Occasionally, double lines of stones

Figure 8-18
Cliffs in winter along Awosting Lake Carriage Road between the crossings of the Long Path and the Blueberry Run Trail.

Figure 8-19
*The Blueberry Run
Trail crosses the
rushing Peter's Kill
on this footbridge.*

direct the walker onto the established path, minimizing wear on the delicate vegetation.

For about a mile, the pine-dotted ledges alternate with areas of thicker soil which are covered with hemlock and birch and interlaced with a network of roots. Past a stream crossing, the trail was rerouted in 1994. Directly ahead is a short yellow-blazed trail which leads directly to the Awosting Lake Carriage Road. Forking right is the new route of the Blueberry Run Trail, which serves to keep the walker from having to follow that much-used road *(Figure 8-18)*. The rerouted trail heads northeast, rising then leveling, and cuts across the route of a well-cleared power line. Here the walker can peer far down across the Rondout Valley and see the Rondout Reservoir nestled amid low hills in front of the far Catskills.

Blueberry Run continues through a veritable canyon of mountain

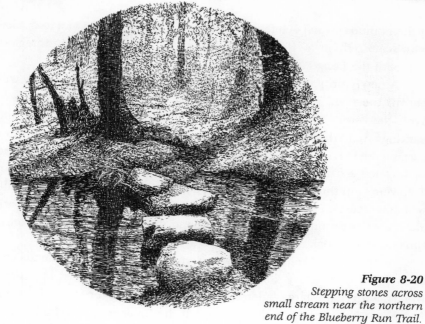

Figure 8-20
Stepping stones across
small stream near the northern
end of the Blueberry Run Trail.

laurel, which reach heights of over ten feet and have stems as thick as four inches. Continuing through this laurel forest, the trail turns down toward the north. Just over two miles from Castle Point, it crosses the Awosting Lake Carriage Road. (To the right, it is 1½ miles to the Lake Minnewaska parking area.) After crossing the carriage road, the Blueberry Run Trail returns to its original route. Reflecting the dip of the underlying conglomerate layers, the trail steepens as it winds through woods dominated by paper birches and crosses an impressive rock exposure. After crossing the new Laurel Trail, Blueberry Run reaches a wooden bridge over the Peter's Kill *(Figure 8-19)*. This lovely stream forms small falls and deep pools as it zigzags over the pebbly, dipping rock layers and rushes under the bridge. It is a fine spot to rest. At about 1,500 feet in elevation, it is the lowest point on the trail.

From the bridge, the trail heads uphill on rough stone steps and crosses the Peter's Kill Carriage Road (to the right, it is about 1½ miles to Route 44-55). Past the well-traveled carriage road, the trail drops slightly to cross a small stream on several well-placed boulders *(Figure 8-20)*.

It then climbs a final 100 feet over ledges to reach the top of a low ridge with scattered views. Here the Blueberry Run Trail ends at an intersection with the Long Path.

A newly-proposed path, to be known as the **Mossy Glen Trail,** will permit the walker from the Awosting parking area on Route 44-55 to avoid the Peter's Kill Carriage Road, so popular with bicyclists. From the parking area, the trail is reached by turning left immediately after passing the barrier gate. Crossing a small brook, the route follows a broad path (once a carriage road) for a short distance. Soon the Mossy Glen Trail veers left through the woods and descends a slope to the Peter's Kill, which it crosses. Following the southeasterly side of the stream, the path alternates between laurel and rhododendron thickets and bare, sometimes slippery rock outcrops.

As the nearby Peter's Kill flows over ledges in a series of rapids and deep pools, the Mossy Glen Trail weaves through the base of a deep woods, with many large fallen hemlocks. In a little over two miles from Route 44-55, it ascends a slope to end at the Blueberry Run Trail. Here, the walker can turn right, cross the nearby bridge over the Peter's Kill, climb up to the carriage road and continue on the trail to intersect the Long Path. Alternatively, one can turn left on Blueberry Run towards Castle Point and another intersection with the Long Path.

9. SAM'S POINT AND VERKEERDER KILL

The southernmost part of the Northern Shawangunks is dominated by a high plateau several miles wide. Except for a few spots near fault lines and along a narrow northwest border zone, the terrain consists of nearly horizontal layers of conglomerate *(Figure 9-1)*. When seen on a topographic map, the plateau edge has a pointed, arrowhead shape. Sam's Point is the tip of the arrow *(see map: Figure 9-2)*. The cliff edge here is the highest in the Shawangunks. The "arrowhead" is honed by the headward erosion of South Gully on the Rondout side of the plateau and the Verkeerder Kill on the Wallkill drainage. The Verkeerder Kill – a shallow, fast-flowing stream – drops over a spectacular waterfall at the edge of the plateau.

The flat, slabby terrain behind the cliff supports an extensive pine barrens. Situated in the barrens are two Sky Lakes: Mud Pond and Lake Maratanza. At 2,245 feet above sea level, Maratanza is the highest of the

Sky Lakes. Mud Pond, the smallest of the lakes, is now part of Minnewaska State Park Preserve and is surrounded by a narrow strip of park land. On some older maps it is called Lake Haseco ("has echo").

The Village of Ellenville owns approximately 4,600 acres of the plateau, including Sam's Point and Lake Maratanza. It uses the lake and North Gully stream for the village's water supply. Lake Maratanza receives

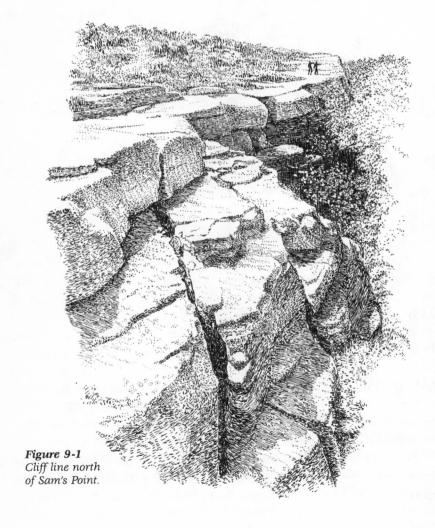

Figure 9-1
Cliff line north
of Sam's Point.

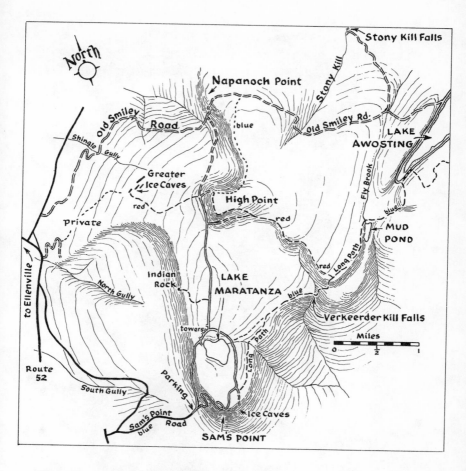

Figure 9-2 *Map of Sam's Point-Verkeerder Kill Section.*

its water only from rainfall, directly and as runoff from the very low slopes around its perimeter. Since it is naturally shallow, the lake has been dredged of bottom sediments in order to maximize its holding capacity.

In 1967, Ellenville leased Sam's Point and the land around Lake Maratanza to a commercial organization which converted the area south of the lake into a tourist attraction, called Ice Caves Mountain. At the edge of the cliff, a section of deep crevices in the conglomerate was fitted with paths, stairways and colored lights to offer an entertaining expe-

Figure 9-3 *Collapsed rock fragments and crevices at the Greater Ice Caves.*

rience for family outings and school groups. The crevices near Sam's Point originated in a manner similar to those at the Rock Rifts *(see Mohonk chapter)*: blocks of conglomerate separating along joint cracks and tilting outward. The cliffs here are the southeastern edge of the conglomerate formation.

On the northwest edge of the plateau, far from this former tourist attraction, there is another group of deep crevices also called "Ice Caves" *(Figure 9-3)*. These may be thought of as the Greater Ice Caves; they were formed along a zone of flexure *(Figure 9-4)* where the conglomerate strata begin to curve downward from near-level layers of the plateau to dip ever more steeply toward the Rondout Valley.

Between 1967 and 1996, when the Ellenville-owned lands were under the control of privately-owned Ice Caves Mountain, Inc., hiking was generally not permitted on this property. In 1996, the Open Space Institute, in conjunction with the Eastern New York Chapter of the Nature Conservancy, acquired the ownership of Ice Caves Mountain, Inc., and these two conservation groups now control most of the land in the southern Shawangunks owned by the Village of Ellenville. Their long-term goal is to have this area added to the Minnewaska State Park Preserve. As of 1997, hiking is again permitted on the Ellenville property, and a number

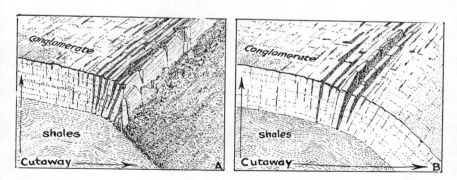

Figure 9-4 Major crevice formations occur in two different places where open crevices or rifts tend to develop: A. The edge of a conglomerate formation where joint-separated sections of rock slump outward; examples are the Rock Rifts and the Sam's Point Ice Caves. B. Zone of flexure where dip angle increases rapidly and conglomerate pulls apart, separating into crevices and wall-like sections; an example is the Greater Ice Caves.

Figure 9-5
Sam's Point.
The road below
is now closed to
vehicular traffic
but open to walkers.

of old and overgrown trails (some described below) have been rejuvenated. However, with the exception of the short trail to Indian Rock, access to the area west of High Point Road – including the Greater Ice Caves – is by permit only. For further information, hikers should write to the Eastern New York Chapter of the Nature Conservancy, Inc., 251 River Road, Troy, N.Y. 12180, or call them at (518) 272-0195.

ACCESS

Sam's Point and the Lake Maratanza area can be reached by driving to Cragsmoor, located southeast of Ellenville and off of Route 52. From just below the crest of Route 52, take Cragsmoor Road to the hamlet of Cragsmoor and then continue on Sam's Point Road to the former Ice Caves Mountain gatehouse. Before 1997, visitors were required to pay a fee here, and could then drive around Lake Maratanza, past the Ice Caves and right to Sam's Point, using a three-mile loop road. This road is now closed to traffic, but hikers may park at the old gatehouse and proceed on foot to the lake or to Sam's Point *(Figure 9-5)*.

For the Mud Pond and Verkeerder Kill Falls region, most visitors used to follow the Long Path south from Lake Awosting. The falls are about six miles from Route 44-55, which means a round trip of approximately 12 miles from the nearest parking areas at Minnewaska State Park. More direct access to Verkeerder Kill Falls was formerly available via the Long Path, which ascended the east side of the Shawangunk escarpment from Upper Mountain (Daschner) Road, reaching the falls by means of a steep, 1½-mile-long climb. This section of the Long Path was closed in the late 1980s, after a change in ownership of the private property below the cliffs. As of 1997, however, much more convenient access to the falls area has become available with the opening of the newly-rerouted section of the Long Path near Sam's Point.

The Greater Ice Caves, three miles north of Sam's Point, are reachable (with a permit) via a faint trail that descends from the old High Point Road (now closed to vehicular traffic) north of Lake Maratanza. They also may be reached via the Old Smiley Road, once a carriage road from Ellenville to Minnewaska, but now an eroded, rocky path. However, it still provides access to hikers from Ellenville to the northwestern slopes of the mountain – especially to Napanoch Point and High Point and, indirectly, to the Greater Ice Caves.

ROADS AND TRAILS

Sam's Point - Ice Caves Region

From Cragsmoor, the **Sam's Point Road** climbs to the old gatehouse and parking lot below the cliffs. Beyond the parking lot, the road (now closed to vehicular traffic) forks left and right. These represent the ends of a three-mile loop, on which one-way vehicular traffic was formerly permitted. The most direct route to Sam's Point is to the right; the left branch heads towards Lake Maratanza. If followed to the left, the road leads past a number of decrepit shacks that once housed berry pickers and basket-weavers. On the right are huge, fallen blocks of Shawangunk conglomerate.

Figure 9-6
*Looking across the largest
of the Greater Ice Caves.*

As the road climbs onto the plateau, various radio towers and antennae come in view to the left. Just beyond them there is a dirt road heading north (left). This is **High Point Road,** an old carriage road that leads to the base of High Point, a hill two miles away. Until recently, High Point was the site of a fire tower that could be seen from afar. In spite of its name, the elevation at High Point is about the same as that of Lake Maratanza.

The High Point area is the focus of a number of old roads and trails once popular with hikers. About a third of a mile along this old road, on the left, is the beginning of the yellow-blazed **Indian Rock Trail.** The first part of this path is muddy but well-cleared; the last part, along a cliff edge, is marked with rock cairns. Three-fourths of a mile from the High Point Road, the hiker reaches Indian Rock, a displaced cabin-size mass of bedrock, shaped by glaciers and picturesquely perched on the cliffs over a deep crevice *(title page illustration)*.

From the Indian Rock Trail, High Point Road continues north, descends to cross a flooded area and, in 1½ miles from the hilltop, reaches the Old Smiley Road. From the base of High Point, an old red-marked trail descends to the west to reach the Greater Ice Caves in about 1¾ miles *(Figure 9-6)*. (As mentioned above, a permit is required to visit this area.) Across the carriage road from this trailhead is a dirt track that climbs to the site of the fire tower, where the **High Point Trail** is encountered. Little used since the advent of the commercial Ice Caves operation, this old blue-blazed trail is being partially rejuvenated. South of the old tower site it will now be marked with red blazes.

Following this newly-cleared trail to the south, the actual summit of High Point (elevation 2,246 feet) is reached in a quarter of a mile. Continuing somewhat easterly, the trail crosses an extensive pine barrens (sometimes called the Slablands or Badlands). Following the irregular edges of low cliffs just above the headwaters of the Verkeerder Kill, the trail finally encounters the Long Path atop a broad, glacially-smoothed outcrop. This trail junction, marked by a rock cairn, is about a quarter of a mile east of Verkeerder Kill Falls.

From the tower site near High Point, the old blue-blazed trail also led in the other direction, eventually heading north towards Napanoch Point. At

Figure 9-7 *Eroded cove in cliff edge near Sam's Point. The cove was worn by torrential meltwaters falling through a crevasse in melting glacial ice over 10,000 years ago.*

this writing, this little-used trail is extremely overgrown and difficult to follow. For the curious and determined explorer, however, the faint trail may still be traced across slab-rock pine barrens – heading first east, then north, and finally descending to the Old Smiley Road just east of Napanoch Point.

After passing the old road to High Point, Sam's Point Road curves around the shore of Lake Maratanza. Although it is the highest of the Sky Lakes, Maratanza is surely the least impressive. No cliffs or prominent outcrops grace the shore, and dredging has left the edges bare and artificial-looking. Beyond the lake, a drive branches to the left, leading to a parking area that was constructed for the nearby Ice Caves. The main road continues ahead to Sam's Point.

Spectacular Sam's Point, at 2,255 feet above sea level, is about 30 feet higher than Castle Point, which is five miles away as the crow flies. There is a fine view over the Wallkill Valley toward the Hudson Valley and beyond. For those daring enough to bypass the unsightly safety wall and follow the cliff edge, a number of interesting crevices and glacial features can be found *(Figure 9-7)*.

Passing the lookout at Sam's Point, the loop road descends below the cliffs and meets its other branch. Just beyond is the gatehouse and parking lot. The distance from the parking lot to Sam's Point by this direct route is about half a mile, with a rise of just over 200 feet.

The **Old Smiley Carriage Road** was built in the late 19th century to provide a route to Minnewaska from the valley to the west. Running from Ellenville to Lake Awosting, this seven-mile-long road rises over 1,600 feet. It required great effort to construct and maintain, with a number of bridges and several sharp switchbacks along the route. The road was used to bring guests and supplies from the railroad and the canal at Ellenville to the Minnewaska Mountain Houses.

By the early 20th century, this side of the mountain had become very popular with blueberry pickers. Groups and families of berry pickers set up a variety of summer camps along the first four miles of Smiley Road, above Ellenville. By the 1950s, the berry pickers had mostly given up, and road maintenance had long been discontinued by Minnewaska. Today there is scarcely a single stretch of the road that is not eroded down to the stone rubble or even to the bedrock below *(Figure 9-8).* Nevertheless, the Old Smiley Road remains an important route for hikers on the southwestern side of the Shawangunks, and the entire right of way is part of the Minnewaska State Park Preserve.

Figure 9-8 *The Old Smiley Road just west of Napanoch Point. Deeply eroded, it has long been impassable to vehicles, and in places even walking can be difficult.*

The lower end of Smiley Road is on the eastern outskirts of Ellenville, near a ballfield and a fire station on Berme Road. From the valley, the old road rises through four switchbacks and crosses the Shingle Gully stream. Shingle Gully Bridge is about half a mile from the Greater Ice Caves, which are some 700 feet higher upslope. About 2½ miles from the beginning of Smiley Road, a faint track forks off the road

Figure 9-9 Pitch pines near Napanoch Point showing characteristic distorted branches.

towards the right. Soon after, the road crosses Beaver Creek, which flows northwest into the depths of spectacular Louis Ravine. Beyond the creek crossing, a dirt road comes in from the right. This is the northern extension of High Point Road. Just ahead on Smiley Road is Napanoch Point, 1,900 feet above sea level.

At Napanoch Point, there are fine views across the Rondout Valley toward the Catskills from an overlook just west of the road and from the slightly higher cliffs to the east. Here, the explorer may find many examples of the distorted and dwarfed pitch pines so characteristic of the Shawangunk ledge terrain *(Figure 9-9)*. Beyond the cliffs, Smiley Road continues southeast, crossing the Stony Kill in 1½ miles and reaching Lake Awosting in about three miles from Napanoch Point.

An interesting hike that includes the Greater Ice Caves can be made from the Napanoch area (a permit is required; see p.159 above). From Napanoch Point, head down Smiley Road a short distance and turn south onto the High Point Road. After crossing Beaver Creek, upstream from

Smiley Road, the walker reaches a flooded region of dead trees and marsh caused by beaver activity. Once past this difficult terrain, the road ascends, steeply in places, to reach the foot of High Point, about a mile from Smiley Road.

To reach the Greater Ice Caves, one must find an old red-marked trail that heads westward, down a gentle slope, from the cleared area at the foot of High Point. Descending more steeply, through mountain laurel and twisted pines, the faded trail reaches the Ice Caves, 1 1/2 miles from High Point *(Figure 9-10)*.

The Greater Ice Caves were produced when conglomerate masses separated along joint cracks. Pulled apart by gravity along this zone of flexure, great sections of gently sloping bedrock moved outward, leaving deep, canyon-like gaps ranging from step-across width to more than a hundred feet across. Ice persists in some of the depths well into the summer, especially where conglomerate slabs bridge over the upper part of the gaps and block the sun.

Figure 9-10 *Entrance to one of the crevices of the Greater Ice Caves.*

Figure 9-11 *Slump blocks along cliff edge near the Long Path.*

Much time can be spent exploring the numerous paths that have developed among the yawning crevices, but extreme caution should be exercised.

An overgrown red-marked trail continues downhill from near the entrance of a very large crevice at the southern edge of the Ice Caves area. The trail is narrow and occasionally difficult to follow as it descends steeply to the west, reaching privately-owned lands and ending at a graded dirt road which eventually leads to Route 52.

Verkeerder Kill - Mud Pond Region

Verkeerder Kill Falls, a gem of the Shawangunks, is a mile from Mud Pond, two miles from the southwestern end of Lake Awosting, and about the same distance from Sam's Point. These sites are connected by a section of the **Long Path.** Mud Pond and Verkeerder Kill Falls have been seldom visited in recent years because the lack of access from the Maratanza-Sam's Point area meant that visitors had to come from Lake Awosting to the northeast. This has now changed dramatically with the opening of the Long Path from near Sam's Point to the falls. Nevertheless,

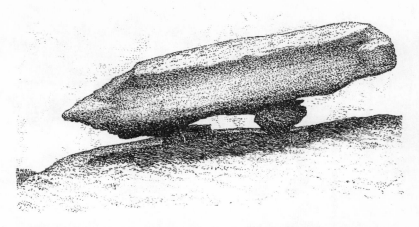

Figure 9-12 *"Balanced Rock," a glacial erratic left by melting ice atop several smaller erratics, in the Crags area south of Mud Pond.*

the route from Lake Awosting continues to provide a splendid variety of Shawangunk landscape features and vistas. The following is a description of the approach to the falls via the Long Path from Lake Awosting.

The turquoise-blazed Long Path leaves the Awosting Shore Road near the south end of the lake, only a few yards beyond the turnoff to Murray Hill. As soon as Lake Awosting is left behind, there is a sense of wildness and remoteness as the trail heads south *(Figure 9-11)*.

Many cairns dot this area, some of which once led around the east side of the pond to a region known as the Crags. This area has a number of short, separated ridges composed of unusually steeply-dipping conglomerate layers. Glacial erratics are abundant on the ridgetops *(Figure 9-12),*

Figure 9-13 *Rock cairns, indicating routes followed by previous hikers, are frequently encountered in the Shawangunks.*

Figure 9-14 *Mud Pond near its outflow – the head of Fly Brook – as seen from the Long Path.*

including some large boulders "balanced" atop smaller ones. Steep, even vertical, dips such as those seen here are rare in the Shawangunks; they indicate the proximity of geological faults. In this case, a major fault zone cuts through the border of the Crags and along Mud Pond. Faintly worn footpaths and deer trails start and stop in the dense growth of blueberry and sheep laurel. "Wildcat" rock cairns – some ruined, some intact – add to the confusion *(Figure 9-13)*. Nevertheless, the Crags area is well worth exploring, but it should be borne in mind that it is not within the Park Preserve boundary.

The Long Path curves around the west side of Mud Pond. It is nearest to the lake on its north side at the outlet, which has been somewhat modified by beaver work. This is the head of Fly Brook, which flows north through miles of wetlands, curving gradually around Lake Awosting *(Figure 9-14)*. North of Lake Awosting, slow-moving Fly Brook meets the rushing outflow from Awosting to form the Peter's Kill.

At the outlet of Mud Pond, a sturdy plank walkway crosses muddy sections of the path. Highbush blueberries along the boardwalk can easily detain a late-summer hiker. Continuing south and past Mud Pond *(Figure 9-15)*, the Long Path gradually ascends onto a long ridge with increasing vistas, including views of the Crags to the east. Along the route here, many cairns compensate for the lack of trees large enough for painted blazes.

About three-fourths of a mile from Mud Pond's outlet, the trail nears the end of a ridge. Sam's Point can be seen ahead. Here, where the Shawangunk conglomerate tends to be relatively fine-grained, there is a biblical inscription, carved long ago into the smooth surface of the bedrock. The painstakingly shaped letters are becoming weathered and lichen-encrusted. Just beyond the inscription is a cairn marking the intersection with the newly-cleared red-blazed trail which leads to High Point (see above).

For the final approach to Verkeerder Kill Falls, the Long Path descends a densely-wooded slope. Ahead is the distant sound of rushing water. The trail cuts through a thicket of mountain laurel and reaches the edge of a great V-cut into the escarpment by the stream. There are several vantage points along the top of the "V" from which to admire the

Figure 9-15 *Glacial boulder on ledges overlooking Mud Pond from the south.*

falls, which truly are a magnificent sight *(Figure 9-16)*. The dropoff is so steep that it may be dangerous to try to get a view of the splash pools 100 feet below.

Until recently, the Long Path was closed beyond this point, leaving a considerable gap in this famous long-distance trail. A new route has now been completed to fill this gap in the Long Path as it continues south to the George Washington Bridge. From Verkeerder Kill Falls, the new segment of the Long Path continues westerly along an historic trail, formerly blazed red. About three-fourths of a mile from the falls, a newly-

Figure 9-16
*Verkeerder
Kill Falls.*

constructed path leaves the well-worn historic route, veering more southerly through an interesting variety of woodland interspersed with open fields. Crossing the outlet stream of Lake Maratanza, the Long Path traverses a moor-like stretch of pine barrens, with sweeping views of the distant Hudson Highlands as well as the Shawangunk escarpment, including Castle Point, Gertrude's Nose and Lake Awosting. About 1½ miles from the falls, the turquoise blazes turn right onto a dirt road which soon reaches Sam's Point Road. The Long Path turns left on this road, which leads to the parking lot near the gatehouse.

For nearly 100 years, the vision of the Smileys has helped safeguard the Shawangunks. Since the 1960s, this role has, in large part, passed to other organizations and individuals. It has been my good fortune to have witnessed during my hiking years an ever-increasing amount of the Shawangunks becoming available for public access. The State of New York and several non-profit organizations – including Mohonk Preserve and Friends of the Shawangunks – have worked to forestall development and to keep large sections of the mountain unchanged and open to hiking and other recreational uses. They have continued to expand upon the Smileys' masterwork of land conservation. Minnewaska State Park Preserve has grown to include three of the Sky Lakes.

One sad exception to this trend was the decrease in access to the Sam's Point and Verkeerder Kill sections of the mountaintop. Historically, these areas have had fewer roads and trails than the more northerly parts of the Shawangunks. In recent years, access to these routes was drastically reduced because of lack of maintenance, private ownership and closed trailheads. Now that the Open Space Institute and the Nature Conservancy have reopened the Lake Maratanza-Sam's Point area to hikers, this broad, splendid area of the Northern Shawangunks is once again available for walking and for other benign recreational uses appropriate to this unique natural environment.

ADDENDUM

As this book goes to press, the Mohonk Preserve's new Visitor Center below the Trapps Cliffs is nearing completion. This new Center is located on Route 44-55 about ½ mile from the well-known "hairpin turn" and near the Trapps Bridge. Information and parking will be available at this location, and a new connecting trail will be built to the Undercliff Carriage Road, which is just uphill from the "hairpin turn." The principal parking area for hiking in this area, however, will continue to be at the large parking lot west of Trapps Bridge, about ¾ mile from the new Visitor Center. A sketch map of the Trapps Bridge-Visitor Center area is below.

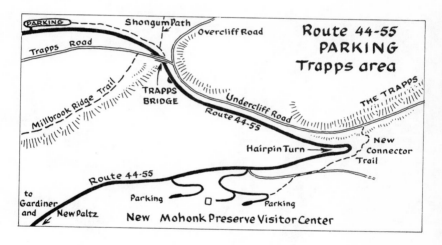

The opening of its new Trapps Bridge location on Route 44-55 will mean that the old Preserve Visitor Center on Mountain Rest Road will be closed by 1998. At this time, it is uncertain whether any parking will be possible near the old Center. If not, the access to trails in the Bonticou area, especially as described on pages 49-53, will be changed considerably. The reader may wish to enter the area from the Spring Farm parking area and should consult the map on page 40.

THE NEW YORK-NEW JERSEY TRAIL CONFERENCE

The New York-New Jersey Trail Conference is a nonprofit federation of nearly 10,000 individuals and 85 hiking and environmental organizations working to build and maintain foot trails and to preserve open space.

The Conference was formed in 1920, and its founders built the first section of the Appalachian Trail in 1923. Today, our hiking trail network includes 1,300 miles of marked trails, extending from the Catskills and Taconics south to the Delaware Water Gap. The Conference is supported by membership dues, publication sales and donations – along with thousands of hours of volunteer time. Members receive the bimonthly *Trail Walker,* can purchase our maps and guides at a 20-25% discount, use the extensive Conference library, get substantial discounts at over 20 outdoor stores and trailside lodges... and more.

Dues start at just $21 ($15 for students, seniors and those with limited income; $26 for a family). For more information, write to us at 232 Madison Avenue, New York, NY 10016, or call (212) 685-9699. You can also contact us via e-mail at nynjtc@aol.com or visit our Web site at: www.nynjtc.org.

INDEX